The Soul on the Ceiling

Conversations on Reincarnation

As told to

Anthea Wynn

The Soul on the Ceiling

Published by Celestial Revelations
PO Box 164
Seddon 3011
Vic Australia
info@celestialrevelations.com
www.celestialrevelations.com
www.antheawynn.com

© 2018 Anthea Wynn

First published in 2018 by Animal Dreaming Publishing, Australia,
animaldreamingpublishing.com

Cover design: WorkingType Studio
Cover image: Falls of the Clyde, JWM Turner

Cataloguing-in-Publication details are available from the National Library of Australia.

ISBN: 978-0-9943078-1-1

All rights reserved. No part of this publication may be reproduced in whole or in part, in any form or by any means without written permission from the publisher, except for the inclusion of brief quotes in a review.

The information in this book is intended for spiritual and emotional guidance only. It is not intended to replace medical advice or treatment.

Contents

Introduction		1
Chapter 1	The soul	5
Chapter 2	The soul at and before birth	18
Chapter 3	The embodied soul	37
Chapter 4	The soul at and before death	68
Chapter 5	The discarnate soul	84
Chapter 6	Walk-ins	100
Chapter 7	Past lives	116
Chapter 8	Ben's journal	140
Chapter 9	Peace on earth…	174
Epilogue		183
Acknowledgements		184

Introduction

"This is I, Saint-Germaine. Welcome and lovely to see you here today. I just wanted to say that I hope you enjoy and can learn from my ramblings all about the soul and past lives throughout this book. I hope this generates a much wider understanding and therefore a greater acceptance of reincarnation as a normality in everybody's life, irrespective of culture."

This is generally how every channelling session with Saint-Germaine starts, with a boisterous welcome full of warmth and encouragement.

Channelling is a form of communication between two energies where one (a human) is the receiver or a conduit for the information, and the other (an invisible being) is the sender; it is a method of receiving messages from an external, invisible source.

Channelling can be likened to tuning into a radio station where each station operates on its own frequency. When a person channels, they are plugging into an individual energy frequency in order to connect to a specific intelligent being. This may link the channeller to a discarnate soul, beings from the angelic realm, ascended masters, spirit guides, even aliens.[1] And like a radio frequency, the channeler is merely the conduit for the messages and may or may not personally believe or accept them.

For practical and safety reasons channelling is best undertaken with two people present, the channeller and a facilitator. The facilitator's job is to ensure the wellbeing of the channeller but if questions are being asked of the spirit which is speaking, then they also become the questioner. Clynton has been my facilitator for this book.

Channelling is not new. Names known to most of us include Nostradamus, who lived in the 16th century producing his prophecies in the form of quatrains. History also tells of Pythia, the Oracle of Delphi in ancient Greece, who was said to channel the sun god Apollo. The best known 20th-century channeller was Edgar Cayce, who produced a corpus of medical diagnoses for ailing individuals. The 21st century seems to have generated a resurgence with names including Neale Donald Walsh (author of the *Conversations with God* book series), Esther Hicks (who channels collective wisdom under the name of Abraham) Geoffrey Hoppe (who runs Crimson Circle) and Lee Carroll (who channels Kryon).

Most channellers need to be in a trance or under hypnosis to be able to channel. I (and I am not unique in this) am able to do this spontaneously by setting the intent that I wish to do this next Tuesday at 3 pm, let's say. At the agreed time my facilitator will be present, I will set up the voice recorder, make myself comfortable, and the process starts almost instantly. What happens is that my soul vacates my body, leaving space for the discarnate speaker to temporarily take up residence. This enables him (and most often it is a male-energy being) to use my physical body (ie my voice and that part of my brain to do with language and emotions) to relay his messages or story. I do not hear and then repeat the messages; they are spoken directly. Coming out of the channelling is the reverse of this, ie the speaker leaves and my own soul returns to my body.

Our sessions are structured with a pre-set purpose; for instance, for this book, we would have a list of questions about souls. Before we start, this intent registers

---

[1] This definition is adapted from the article *What is Channelling* by Tracie Delysia Wolter, first published in 2015 in *International Psychics Directory*.

with the specific being we need to fulfil this objective and usually, he will come through first. Quite often other spirits will follow with additional material. I have no control over who comes through or the order in which they appear and I have never experienced any mischievous or malevolent spirits. I can only channel one being at a time.

Lastly let me explain that in order to differentiate my comments from Saint-Germaine's answers, I have used this typeface for my words, whereas his explanations (in a different font) follow the questions, which are in italics. There are also occasional human stories to illustrate a particular point. These are in a different font again.

Saint-Germaine, Ben and friends

Let me introduce the book's characters, the storytellers, all of whom are discarnate beings:

Saint-Germaine is an ascended master (and he is one among many). These are senior souls who have a support and guiding role in helping less-evolved souls. Saint-Germaine is also one of my spirit guides which is why he has worked with us on this book. He answered our myriad of questions, all of which makes up the bulk of this book.

Ben is a male-energy soul who has had a two-thousand-year gap since his last life. He was fascinated by modern technology and wanted to return to experience this for himself. He also wanted to tell us his soul-planning journey because nobody has ever previously given progress reports as this process unfolded. This is Chapter 8.

Daniel is a soul who shared Ben's most recent past life. In that life, Daniel was Ben's father and he has not reincarnated since.

Gabriel is an archangel (and there are many of them too) which is the angelic equivalent of an ascended master. Although archangels are often considered a Christian concept, they are also important figures in other religions including Judaism and Islam.

Why tell this story now

At the end of a session in May 2015, Ben offered this explanation:

I'm just a contact who has come through because I was aware that you were channelling. I can tell you that many, many people up here are aware that you have been channelling, in part because you have been doing it so consistently for all these years. It was they collectively who wanted to use you as an opportunity to tell this story. That's how it came about.

Later on Gabriel (as the spokesperson for a collective of senior beings) gave us some additional background:

The idea [of telling his planning story] came from Ben asking you two about computers. Then dear old Saint-Germaine, I have to give him ten out of ten, he was the one who said I wonder if this lad is planning a new incarnation. From that, we joined the dots. Anthea could channel, Ben was very happy and comfortable talking to you both, so wouldn't it serve if Ben told his story? We suggested this and he was more than willing to keep talking to you. He did wonder if there would be bits he didn't want to say. We said, "If that's the case then it's totally your prerogative and let's face it, they will never know and the questions will never be asked."

We genuinely want to spread the word [about reincarnation]. So many people are petrified of death and we want to allay that fear by reassuring them that life continues afterwards. It was we collectively who encouraged Ben to undertake this project. I have to say in retrospect, I'm really glad we did.

Chapter 1

THE SOUL

This book is an encyclopaedic collection of questions and answers about the human soul, reincarnation and past lives; all the answers have been channelled from Saint-Germaine.

The word reincarnation derives from the Latin literally meaning to enter the flesh again. The concept pre-dates Socrates, is a basic tenet of Buddhism and features in many religions and philosophies across the world.

At its most simple, the idea behind reincarnation is that a soul comes back, time after time, into a new physical body (sometimes male, other times female) to live another life with the purpose of learning new, or more, lessons. This cycle can repeat hundreds, even thousands, of times, with gaps between each life ranging from next-to-nothing to thousands of years.

To help you understand let me summarise a number of concepts that Saint-Germaine has given:

- a soul is pure energy and therefore gender-neutral,
- every living human, from conception to death has a soul, even if death occurs in-utero, at birth or early childhood,

- every soul comes into a new life with a plan and goals, and then to experience events which will allow it to meet these objectives,
- every soul returns after death to review the life that has just ended to see if it met its goals,
- a soul is eternal; ie it never dies or ends.

What is the word for the place where the soul lives when it's not incarnate?

We can't use heaven because that's a Christian concept. Ether is probably a good word. I know you folk have coined the phrase 'on the other side of the veil.' It's a nice expression because the veil is the human form. Veils and clouds make you forget; but in Islam, veil has a different connotation and we don't want to get complicated.

Perhaps an invisible eternity, an infinite, infinity… no, that's a mathematical concept where infinity is a point that goes forever so that's not what we mean. An infinite invisible realm which incorporates all the space in the whole universe.

While humankind believes this universal space to be empty, it's actually full of souls and beings and entities and spirits (whatever word you wish to use). By definition, they are invisible to the human eye.

I think that infinite invisible realm defines it but in general conversation, we can't keep using that rather long phrase all the time. We love the word 'upstairs.' It's kind of jokey but it's sincere. We all understand upstairs and downstairs in houses. If you wanted to keep using the word upstairs, it's a simple concept which everyone recognises.

The phrase 'up here' is also used sometimes and this is really just an alternative for upstairs. If I was asked where this 'up here' is, I would have to say it is the universal empty space, the infinite invisible realm that I have just talked about.

What is a soul? What are its qualities, characteristics, when it's upstairs and is that different from when it's down here? Which and why are human qualities carried back when it passes?

All right, what's a soul? The only way I can think to express it is to say that the soul is the very essence of a human. It is pure energy. It's a collection of energies of different frequencies, each of which creates a human's individual qualities. By that I mean that one frequency might be intelligence, another might be a sense of humour, and so on. Every individual has a unique mix of these qualities and in varying amounts. For example, if a soul had a higher than average intelligence, then the amount of that specific frequency energy would be greater than in most other souls. If someone was very caring and their role in life or lives had been a nurse for example, even to the extreme of going to war to care for the wounded, the percentage of caring energy in that soul will be higher.

These different energies all coalesce or clump together and stay together forever, always. You could draw a circle, a bubble, with an outer edge and I don't mean a hard, physical edge but an outer boundary, which holds this collection of frequencies together. This works in a way that is similar to how the forces within an atom hold that structure of electrons in their orbit around the nucleus; similarly, these energies hold together in these particular ratios to create this unique soul.

A soul will usually have a predominance of what we recognise as male or female energies, qualities which are obvious when it is resident in a human.

A soul exists, survives; the energy exists forever. It is eternal. It never dies and it only gets born in the sense of a human incarnation.

How is a soul created?

First, you might ask – how do those energies within a soul come into existence in the first place?

Every soul is a spark or a spit (perhaps that's not a nice word) from God. God spits out souls, not in a nasty 'spitty' way, more like the way a fire generates sparks. Let's say a soul is like an ember from a hot fire, so in that way, a soul is created by God.

Now you can ask me all you like, how God defines that spit or soul. Nobody can possibly ever answer that question. We just accept there are souls and that they come with a unique composition and complement of qualities and they retain those qualities and that composition forever.

Two questions arise from that then – does a soul's composition change and, does it change over time?

In essence, no – pardon the pun! The composition is largely made up of qualities you would recognise as human traits: love, compassion, hate, anger, fear, what you call evil, caring, intellect, leadership. There's a nearly endless list of human characteristics which will be the big pot from which a new soul is created.

For example, if a soul – we'll call him Joe – has no leadership abilities, that's not a detriment. That's just how God has defined Joe because I assume, God wants to experience what it's like to go through existences on earth for someone who is never going to be a leader. Joe will go through his life being a follower but he will have other attributes.

Let's say that because he's a follower, he might be a strong carer and therefore might make a good mother and grandmother. He might make a really good male nurse, all kinds of different caring things but he would never make a General for example.

Out of the complete pot of all the qualities that are available, not everybody has everything – if they did they probably would be perfect. And Islam has got that right – only God is perfect.

When the soul incarnates the whole bubble comes in by definition. There are enough qualities within that soul that some will be relevant to this life and different ones will be relevant in another life. You don't use all of them every time. If this time you have come to do service then qualities like dominance or humour perhaps, will be dormant. They will still be there but they will not be strong or significant.

Every soul in existence has its own unique blend of qualities in its own particular ratios. Now the question is – does that change over time? By time, I mean aeons.

If a soul only does one incarnation, it still has the opportunity to learn an enormous amount. Regardless of whether it's over one or many lives, let's assume the soul does learn – and this is not a given. A soul can also come to earth with this opportunity to learn and not make the most of that at all. It then returns not much further on than when it left.

When a human dies and the soul returns, those learnings are incorporated into its returning energy bubble. If there are no learnings or it has only learnt a small amount, then that also goes back as a part of the package.

What happens to a newly created soul – does it go to celestial kindergarten or does it come in fully fledged and ready for an incarnation?

Love it! Celestial kindergarten is a fabulous phrase! I've never thought about it, ever!

It does not go celestial kindergarten, no. It's much more like an animal in your world which, within a very short space of time after birth, is fully operational. I know you see television programs with new-born deer for instance, which are standing and walking within minutes.

That's a good analogy. Within a short space of time, souls are up and fully fledged. These are the ultimate in young souls. Because they have no experience or knowledge they spend early times getting to know how things work up here. They are assigned to a guide or guides, your equivalent of a parent except that this guide is more like a mentor.

Unlike parents, they will not dictate the rules and teach them how society works over the years. It is up to the newly-created soul to work with its mentors to ask questions and be guided by their answers. It's not really kindergarten but it is a learning phase they go through until both the soul and the mentors feel that it has gained enough knowledge of existence up here, to start thinking about where it might want to have its first existence – which is not necessarily on earth – and what it might want to do. Once it has made that transition it will start its soul-planning process the same as any other soul.

There are specialists, groups of first-time-round mentors for souls approaching their first incarnation or existence.

What sort of pattern does a soul follow through a typical life?

Through everyday life with its ordinary activities, even as a child, the soul will experience small waves. Today you're lying in your cot but you're unhappy because you've got a wet nappy, so there will be a little down-wave. Then you get your food and you will be calm again so the wave will flatten out. The graph would have waves in it in line with the ups and downs of ordinary things.

Let's say you're a teenager now. In school, the teacher is saying that yours was the best essay in the class. You'll beam and think, "wow, isn't that fantastic," so there'll be a bigger up-wave. If in the gym class the teacher says (well she wouldn't really say) aren't you hopeless at something, then there would be a real drop because it's a big negative.

The soul goes through life like this. Now we all get many ordinary ups and downs every day, things like I didn't like that dinner last night, I don't enjoy the company I'm with right now, or I really appreciated that movie. Mixed in with all that there will be the big exceptions which can be both positive and negative.

Let's say that you're an adult now. The day you get married should be a huge positive. There will be a big up-wave which rises gradually because it's been long in the planning. But on the actual day and at the minute the celebrant says you are now husband and wife it might be a big spike upwards. Wow! This is a huge emotional moment. That's one example. The birth of the first child or the children is something similar.

Let's say the marriage all goes badly wrong and this soul goes through a long period of painful, hurtful experiences. There would be a lot of downs through that experience. Let's say that eventually, the relationship ends. That might be a huge downer on one hand because you never wanted that to happen but on the other hand, it might be accompanied by a huge up because it's a relief that it's over. There can be both sides.

When an event is unexpected and the human is unprepared for it, then you'll get a sudden sharp spike. The extreme is, of course, your own unexpected death. A lesser extreme will be an unexpected death or serious illness of someone important to you. If you're suddenly told that your mother, who you are very close to, has got cancer that would generate a big negative down, a horrid spike. Over the next days or weeks that spike will slowly come back up as you get used to the idea. Then as Mother makes a recovery so you'll get more upward blips because this is all now becoming positive again.

Something like an unexpected and unwanted pregnancy will be another big negative spike… "*oh my god*, what am I going to do?" It's really around this issue of being unexpected and traumatic. Conversely, if somebody tells you something wonderful, which is unforeseen like a long-standing friend has won the lottery, then that's an unexpected positive spike. It's all to do with the unexpected but the worst ones are the traumas.

What is an old soul? Is there such a thing as a new soul and what about the middle-aged soul?

I love it! The logic is brilliant. Serious question, serious answer.

There are two elements to this; it's almost two dimensional. A soul can be measured in how long since it was spit out, created. (Let's use the word created; I don't like this spitty word.) Alongside that is how much has it developed. By that, I mean achieved the goals it set itself in the various lifetimes, whenever and wherever those lives may have been. An old soul is likely to have had a long time since its creation has also achieved many of its goals through its incarnations. A young soul is likely to be the opposite; relatively recently created and because it's not been around as long, it's had less chance to learn and achieve its goals. Middle-aged ones are anywhere in between.

It's all fluid. It's possible to have an old soul in terms of length of time since its creation, which has still achieved only the same amount of lessons as a young soul which has only been around for a tenth of the time. Just because you've been in existence for aeons it doesn't necessarily follow that you have learnt heaps.

Old souls which are respected have been coming back in recent times with the aim of trying to help earth find some balance in all the unrest and unsettled existence that it's experiencing at the moment. These are souls which are old in both age and wisdom. (That's a lovely word). Because they've reached their goals, they've achieved the learnings associated with them and so they have the wisdom. Mature in years and mature in wisdom.

Now, this leads on to the question – do souls age through time alone up here? The short answer is no.

In your human terms, ageing is a process of deterioration of the physical which is measured by the passing of the years. Since a discarnate soul doesn't have a physical body and we don't measure time at all let alone in the way that humans do, then no, the soul doesn't age. It can only mature in the way I have just described. In between incarnations, it might have learnt more things up here in which case it has matured a bit more, but that is the only way its maturity or wisdom can alter.

What is an advanced soul?

I think it's a terminology issue. I would say an advanced soul is just another way of expressing what we've just described as an old soul.

Can you explain the different levels of soul development?

There aren't really set stages. Is it Buddhism or Hinduism that has you stepping up so that if you do good things you go up to the next level? [Hinduism.]

That strikes me like you're stepping up a set of stairs and it's certainly not as concrete as that. It's all energy and all fluid. A river is a wonderful example. It flows and the further downstream it gets, the more mature it gets. Same thing with a soul; it's all to do with how much learning it will achieve in any incarnation. The more it learns, the more it grows and develops and matures, and so the more wisdom it acquires and the more advanced it is. That steppy concept is a bit misleading.

Can anything harm or be detrimental to a soul?

Isn't that a fabulous question! I think you have to say – what do we mean by harm or being detrimental?

Nothing can physically hurt a soul but can there be energies, emotions or intellectual activities that might harm it? Well, I haven't ever really considered this so let's try and think it through.

The most extreme thing that can happen to a human is to be killed unexpectedly. The second-most extreme thing is to be really badly injured unexpectedly. Both of those are huge shocks to the body, to the emotions and to the intellect. With an unexpected death, the soul is catapulted out in shock, doesn't know what's happened, is confused, what's going on, where am I? I was down there being a soldier on the Western Front two seconds ago. What happened?

With a drastic injury – and car or industrial accidents come to mind mostly these days – there's a huge amount of shock. The soul might be jolted, like "*aaghh*, what's happened?" but not hurtled out of the body. It will be asking, "what's going on; I don't understand." If a lot of blood is lost, it will realise that there's a real risk of death. If there are mangled bones, there will be an excruciating amount of pain, all of which are different physical and emotional reactions for the soul to experience.

Under those conditions, the soul goes into high alertness because all of a sudden there's a vastly increased chance that this physical body will die soon and unexpectedly. It becomes vigilant asking, "do I have to suddenly get ready to leave?" The ambulance will come quickly and the paramedics will undoubtedly be extremely efficient but sometimes they arrive too late. The soul is in watchfulness mode as well as absorbing the experience of this pain and anguish and all the *oh-my-god* reactions that any human would suffer under those circumstances.

If the injuries are so great that the physical dies, then the soul drifts slowly out, unlike the instant unexpected death where it is catapulted out.

It's had a wee bit of warning, even if it's only for ten minutes or half an hour, while those injuries have deteriorated to the point of death. The soul has had that time to go from being alert and aware to realising that this might suddenly be the end. It's not quite as traumatised as the poor soldier, who has been shot in the back. It will come back a bit surprised, a bit 'this wasn't on my plan; what's going on', but because of that short period of preparation, it won't be so freaked out.

So can anything really be detrimental to the soul? I don't think so. You can't overheat it, you can't boil it to death, you can't burn it, you can't put a sword through its heart, you can't do anything to it. While it's a fabulous question, I really think the answer is no. It can't be harmed up here either because we don't do judgement so it doesn't get offended or upset or grumpy or have a hissy fit because we just don't have those things.

The other side to that question must be – is there anything that can be beneficial to a soul?

Well, that's a good question too. I think the answer is only in the same way as beneficial things happen on earth really. If somebody helps you do something then you experience gratitude and thank-yous. Same up here.

So the answer to both questions must be no.

Are there such things as bad or malevolent spirits?

On the whole, the answer is no for souls which incarnate as humans on the earth-plane. At the extreme, people who commit anti-social behaviours like murder and rape, have acquired these traits from human learning, not from the incoming soul. This learning might have arisen from any number of situations, home and parental influences, school environment, falling into with the wrong company, drugs which affect the thinking, even cultural contexts.

If all souls are energy, why do angels, for example, Gabriel, have wings?

It's a human construct. Angels are energy just like everybody else and they are souls in the same way. They don't need physical wings. Your understanding of Gabriel, with his big wings and the softness and comfort and support that they bring, signifies wings on a higher being who is all good.

Angels are generally perceived as bringers of comfort and support. This construct goes back hundreds and thousands of years into art and has become a norm in Western culture. If you asked an ancient Chinese man what he thought about angels, he might say something quite different.

Yes, it's a human construct but it's a lovely way of physically illustrating the concepts of comfort and support and help and guidance.

Do animals have souls and if so are they different from human souls?

Animal souls are largely collective. By that I mean if you have the cat family, all the way from lions and tigers right down to tabby cats, they will have a collective consciousness or a collective soul. All animals, and this is the big difference from humans, operate from instinct and maybe some intuition.

Look at the life of any animal. It grows up, it learns to survive and be self-sufficient. It finds a partner or partners depending on the species; it produces offspring. It keeps eating and hunting to eat and sometimes it will be hunted itself and it just goes around that cycle. That's all it does. The fundamental difference between all animals and humans is… free-will. Only humans have conscious free will, conscious choice.

A lion or cheetah on the African plains, for instance, will say to itself, "I see that antelope." Its instinct will kick in. "My belly is empty and I'm hungry. I chase; I kill; I eat." It doesn't stop to think there's a bigger antelope over there and I'll go for that instead. It's like putting on a pre-programmed loop. Whereas a human might rationalise, "but over here is a nicer piece of food which might be easier to reach, so I'll make a conscious, deliberate choice to go for this better one."

Animals do not have any conscious free choice. That then says they don't need individual souls. They don't have soul plans. Because they don't have a conscious thinking mechanism in the way that humans do, they don't get into the concepts of right and wrong or good and bad. They just exist. They live to do the things they are biologically pre-programmed to do: eat and feed and procreate and sleep and breathe and kill or be killed. The soul is there to keep that instinctive momentum going. Since they've all got the same instinct for the same process, one collective soul works for all.

Now a giraffe family is going to operate differently from say, a mouse family species, so they have different souls to reflect their different needs. But all cats, even domestic tabby cats pretty much operate in the same way at the fundamental functional level. Even a tabby cat can turn feral.

So the answer to the unasked question, do humans ever come back as animals, is basically no for that clear reason.

Chapter 2

THE SOUL AT AND BEFORE BIRTH

As you will see in the following chapters, before every incarnation, the soul prepares a plan which defines its learning goals and objectives for this coming life. When it returns after death, it has a rest and recovery period before reviewing the life that has just ended.

At the start of each new life, we forget all our previous lives so that we can learn afresh by working on a blank canvas.

How do the vast majority of souls who come in through normal healthy births, choose their parents?

The soul will start looking for its parents usually after the mother is pregnant because that is the only time it can be totally certain of the gender of the newborn. There is no point selecting these parents over here whose child will be a girl when you want to come into a boy.

Firstly, there can be any number of variations to this process depending on the complexity of the soul's objectives. Just to illustrate let's say that it wants to return to experience being a gay Sioux with same-sex parents! The likelihood of ever being able to meet those requirements is very remote and so the process of choosing – and waiting for – such an outcome is likely to be a big variation on the norm. Unlike that extreme, what I am about to describe is the path that the vast majority of souls follow to find conventional Mums who will deliver a healthy baby. This is a top-down process which reduces the number of potential candidates at each step. This can take months or even years in your human terms particularly if it is a complicated match.

- Firstly, the soul plan has to be complete, or at least this aspect of it is complete, otherwise, the soul doesn't have a profile of the personal characteristics for matching to their parents.

- Next, the soul chooses its siblings and I will describe that process in a minute. They then work together to find parents who they hope will create the opportunities for all of them to meet their goals for this next life.

- The next consideration is the mother and because it is the mother who does the physical birthing, she is the primary focus. The choice here arises from the vast ocean of all the mothers right across the world who are currently pregnant with a healthy foetus. Mothers whose foetuses are likely to be stillborn, aborted or have a disability are outside the range of candidates, as are mothers carrying multiple foetuses, simply because our soul seeks a single healthy foetus. The soul will know when it makes that choice that the mother is very, very likely to be able to carry that child through to full term and give birth to a healthy child. And the vast majority of mothers do that in every culture.

But you also have to ask – what about the mother's genes?

This is obviously a consideration at this stage but these are probably less important than the father's genes. The reason for saying this is that the vast majority of mothers are pregnant willingly and they really want to be Mums. So their focus and lifestyle, at least for the next few years, will be caring for and raising the baby and looking after hubby and home. All terrific family support qualities and even if she returns to work, her priority will still be the family.

- The next consideration is the sex of the child. At this stage just by the law of averages roughly halves the number of potential candidates.

- After that, the choice is gay or straight. Since the vast majority of newborn infants are straight, only a very small percentage of potential mothers are excluded here.

- Next, comes the choice of culture and country and here the place will follow after the choice of culture. If the soul's plan included living a fairly strict adherence to a Muslim life, then it is more likely to choose a Middle-eastern Arabian country rather than a European-based cross-cultural community where its life would likely be influenced by these neighbouring cultures and peoples.

- The father is the next consideration. He must be able to provide genes which will generate the human characteristics that will provide the opportunity for the soul to meet its goals. For instance, if the soul chooses to experience intellectual challenges then he must choose a father with a highly developed intellect so that when the child, children, challenge his views and opinions then the souls, the siblings, can have that experience. This could also include the opposite experience, ie the opportunity to learn how to avoid this type of behaviour.

- Lastly, the family circumstances are considered. By this stage, the soul is down to the detail of choosing whether it wants to grow up on a farm or in an inner city, whether it wants partnered conventional parents, a stable environment or the likelihood of a family breakdown, poverty or relative affluence, all those sorts of practical material things.

If we'd had this conversation say fifty or more years ago, I would have just said that this part of the choice would be to take the father into account because, nine times out of ten, they would be a stable married couple. There always has to be a biological father of course, but in this day and age they are not necessarily married (which is usually of no consequence to the incoming soul), there is IVF, in vitro fertilisation, there are single mothers and same-sex couples who want to adopt. Although all of these require a father's sperm, that is only part of the consideration these days.

If the soul plan is to grow up in a happy and healthy childhood, in a conventional family relationship, then there is a great deal of choice. If its soul plan says it wants the experience of being brought up by a single mother then that consideration seriously narrows the choices. Although there are plenty of them these days, for every single mother there are still thousands of conventional couples. If it wants a same-sex couple then the choice is even smaller. If it has chosen a culture of a small group of ethnic peoples that, at an extreme is still isolated from the rest of the world, then there is likely to only be one standard lifestyle for that community. This last consideration then becomes redundant of course.

Although I have depicted this as a linear process for ease of understanding, it may be that at some stage a soul, like my gay Sioux wanting same-sex parents, finds that it is not going to be able to fulfil its ideal choice for a very long time if ever. Its soul plan might have other, possibly subsidiary but never the less important goals which are easier to achieve in a shorter time frame. In that case, it may well go back around the loop and start again with a new or amended profile for its parents.

There are no rules that say the soul must stick to this path that I've outlined, nor are there any fixed timescales for achieving it. Just as some souls will take many years finalising their soul plans, so they might also take years finding the right parents, particularly when sibling needs have to be taken into consideration as well.

How do parents choose a name for the new baby and soul? Does the soul communicate its preferences to the parents?

That's a really good question and there are several parts to the answer. One part is obviously when the parents choose family names that they wish to pass onto the next generation and that is often to the sons. That is clear and self-explanatory.

On the whole, parents will only start looking seriously at names when they are fairly certain that the pregnancy will progress to full term. Sometimes these days the parents will know the gender, other times not, so they will likely have a list for both genders.

Every soul will come in with a clear view about what it wants its name to be. Because it knows that this future child is going to be a male, it will only have a small number of boys' names on its list. Souls are usually very clear about what they want to be called.

The parents will go through the mechanics of creating their lists but somewhere along the line, the soul will subtly communicate its preference through the mother for obvious physical reasons. Whether the soul has slipped on board or not, it will still communicate through the foetus into the mother's head – and don't ask me about the mechanisms – that I really want to be called (say) Peter.

If the father (and more often it is the father) is insistent about the family name then a compromise might be reached where both that name plus the soul's preference are used. Occasionally the family name is the same or similar enough to the soul's choice that both parties are happy. The soul will always try to achieve its preferred name but will also know full well that in these cases there is an equal chance that it will fail. It will just live through that life regardless of this.

You could then ask – why would a soul choose a specific name?

It's all to do with the energies around that name as perceived by the soul rather than any human connotations. If you take the name Peter, Christian-based societies will associate him with the Bible, Muslim folk will say something else and a Bushman of the Kalahari will say that it has no meaning for him at all. Although the name itself has a cultural context, this is not usually part of the reason that the soul makes that choice.

How do you choose your siblings?

As part of your planning process, you will discuss with other souls up here (who you may or may not have shared past lives with) what your goals are in this family relationship. It may be to overcome antagonism, or become closely bonded again, or learn to get on with the opposite sex as children because you've only had past lives with same-sex siblings, any number of reasons. Even if it's only two siblings, you all agree that you will incarnate through the same mother to create the opportunity to meet these goals that each of you has set.

They have to make this agreement before the first-born incarnates so they can then go through the process of selecting their parents together. When it comes time for the subsequent siblings to incarnate, the parents are already known and are in place, so they can just hop on board the foetus at whatever time suits their soul plans. To illustrate:

> James is a soul with a slightly aggressive nature and he comes back into a family with two girls and he's the only boy. He might have a need to prove himself as the alpha male in childhood and his way of manifesting those needs is to push the buttons of both his sisters.
>
> Their challenge is how to resist, stand up to him, stand on their own feet and not go into cringe mode but to learn to react assertively and appropriately. Those three siblings will not be close and would not be a karmic group but they have all agreed to come back in this family unit to learn these different traits. That is fairly common.
>
> James becomes an adult who eventually marries a lady who has several sisters all of whom are as close as can be. They almost live in each other's houses and are super-supportive of each other's children. They're a karmic group for family-support type reasons; just to do the nice family things like care and look after and be concerned about other members of the group and their offspring – and their husbands of course, who are not members of this karmic group. By marrying this lady James has chosen to have the opposite experience and relationship from that which he had with his sisters.

Finding a set of two or three siblings is fairly straightforward; where they want to be a group of ten or a dozen, much harder and it obviously takes much longer. Luckily this doesn't happen so often these days.

What happens to the soul during a normal birth?

At the start of the physical process, there's the point of conception. The mother goes through the nine months with more or less ease. Any problems are all physiological to do with the mother's physical situation. The birth happens more or less on time and more or less naturally and the child is born healthy in every sense.

At some point, the soul joins the physical. Firstly, this process is all fluid because the soul is all energy. There's no rule that says the soul will only join at the instant of birth. There are no rules about any of this so it's largely up to the soul and its plan.

The earliest that a soul is likely to join is a week or two after conception. At any point through the nine months, it's perfectly possible for the soul to slip in and be part of the growing foetus along for the ride and the experience at that stage.

The latest point at which a soul is likely to join is a week or two after the birth and again, it's always because of what's in its soul plan. The soul might not wish to experience the rigours of the physical birth. It might wish to let the child become more settled in its new environment, the physical world, before it joins. It's totally a soul's choice and discretion but the norm would be anything from very early on in the pregnancy to let's say, tops, a couple of weeks after the birth.

That then begs the question – for those first two weeks of life, does this living human have a soul?

What happens in is that the soul will be around and connected to the infant in an awareness sense. It will be alert to what's happening with the baby. If something suddenly happened that was going to be an experience it wanted to have, it would just hop on board. It's not floating off in the ether somewhere and not interested or involved. It just hasn't physically slipped in, that's all.

What about a caesarian section?

No different really from a normal birth from the soul's perspective. It's just an alternative method of birthing the foetus, the child.

The soul is not affected by heavy sedation either and a water birth or any other form of birthing would be the same as I have described for a normal birth.

If a foetus develops physical or mental disabilities while it's still in utero, how does this affect the soul?

Let's assume that the foetus goes through to full term and those disabilities are not picked up through the pregnancy. The child is born with some physical or mental problem which may or may not be obvious at birth. Things like blindness and deafness are often not picked up initially and mental function particularly is not picked up till much later. So the questions then are – what is the soul doing and why is this going on?

Well, again, for its own reasons a soul will choose to experience what it is like to be a disadvantaged human, even as an infant.

A soul might choose to join this embryo when it's still developing or at any time through the pregnancy or even after the birth. Because it has chosen to experience a disability it's much more likely to slide into the physical at the time of, or fairly immediately after, the birth. If the disability is bad enough then the child might not survive very long. If the child lives on to adulthood, then that's all part of the experience for the soul.

When it was preparing its plan, the soul decided that it wanted the experience of a physically disadvantaged life and the question then becomes – at what point does the soul know that a particular foetus is going to be disabled?

This is generalising but some disabilities are the result of the conception and others are due to physical conditions imposed during the pregnancy – it might be food, it might be bad air, it might be physical trauma, all manner of things could adversely affect the development of the foetus.

If it's a standard birth and a healthy child, a soul will pick Joan over here to be her new mother. It will all go according to plan because the birth and the child are normal. But when is it able to say that Margaret over there, her foetus has become disabled and I will choose her? God

For all the people who are born disabled – and there will be thousands upon thousands all over the world – there must be an equal number of souls who wish to have this experience. There must be some sort of monitoring and matching mechanism up here where somebody suddenly says, "Ah-ha, Sally over there, her child looks like becoming disadvantaged in some fashion. Here's an opportunity." Then a specific soul will say, "OK, I'll be with Sally's baby."

Once that match has been made, then it's up to the individual soul to decide at what point it wishes to join physically. So there's a slightly different process with disabled children who go through to full term of pregnancy and are born because they still survive into the human world even if it's just for a short time.

What happens with a stillbirth or miscarriage?

Stillbirths and miscarriages are an extension from a disabled foetus because usually a foetus is stillborn or miscarries because there is something physically wrong.

The question then becomes – does that stillborn or miscarried foetus have a soul?

The answer is sometimes yes and sometimes no, which sounds like a cop-out, but it's not. Sometimes a soul will decide it wants that experience of being miscarried or stillborn.

Now from a human perspective that sounds absolutely bizarre. But a soul might decide it just needs a tiny touch of the human physical world, maybe eight or ten weeks in-utero. It might move in right after conception and stay there for that short two or three months, or whatever it happens to be, until the miscarriage or the stillbirth happens.

With a stillbirth the baby has died, so, therefore, would the soul have passed?

Once the foetus has died, the mother usually will be very aware because things have changed. The stillbirth will then happen either naturally or by medical intervention very quickly after the death of the foetus. Even if that happens at three or four months, there's still been that period of living foetus which the soul has experienced.

Then you've got to say – at what point does the soul leave when the foetus dies?

With a stillbirth, the physical foetus has died and the soul will have left at or just before the point of death because it knows that death is imminent. It will say, "I have achieved what I needed to achieve in this short existence, and that's the end of it. I'm leaving." A soul will not still be in situ to experience a physical stillbirth or medical intervention.

I have great difficulty accepting the process…

From a human perspective, I totally understand your reservations. The soul can come and go at will. Souls come and go most night-times when you're asleep so this is no different. It's not like this embryo is doing anything except growing and feeding; it's not even breathing. The heart's pumping but that's about all – and if it's early on it's not even doing that. Because the soul is just energy it can blend in at any stage, have the experience that it's chosen to have and, in some cases, it chooses this incredibly short taster of human existence.

Does the same thing happen during an abortion?

Basically yes, because an abortion is the same end result as a stillbirth or a miscarriage. But there are two differences – it has been manipulated and it's what the mother intended. With a stillbirth or a miscarriage, there was never any intent or wish on the part of the parents. With an abortion, there is, so that's the first difference. There is an intent to end the life of this embryo.

From the point of view of the soul of the child, the process is likely to be the same as I just described for a miscarriage. The soul will join very early on and it will stay for the duration, however short that is, until the abortion happens. The soul will know jolly well that Tuesday next week is the day set for this operation and it will take its leave at some point before that.

With the case of an abortion, the mother or the parents will say, "I don't want this," right from the minute she knows she's pregnant. The intent is there from the beginning to not give birth to a healthy living child that they would then rear to full adulthood. Going back to the mother's soul energy components, there is now an added dimension of intent that she carries.

The question, of course, leads on to – are we killing a living human?

I think that is so complex that I'm not really sure it's appropriate in this book to get into the politics, the ethics, the morality and the integrity around that issue. Having an abortion is very personal and very individual and not always an easy decision.

The other part of the question is – what happens to the soul if a healthy embryo grows and develops into the foetus, but somewhere along the line, it is discovered to have, let's say spina bifida, a deformity that would mean the child was permanently disabled?

Let's also say that this was discovered during all the checks that happen through the pregnancy. Then the mother or the parents decide to terminate the pregnancy.

Well, that's a form of abortion but it's done with different intent. It's not done from the selfish intent of, "I don't want a child." It's usually done after much anguish and soul-searching on the part of the parents because they do want the child, but...

They feel they don't have the fortitude or the requirements to bring that child up properly...

Some of that, and sometimes they don't wish to inflict a life of disability on their child. Sometimes they don't have the money as well as the fortitude to support a disabled child. Sometimes they already have several other children and it would just become a hugely disproportionate load of care on the family and the finances. There are a number of reasons why they would choose to have a termination under those conditions.

It's done with intent by the mother or the parents but it's done out of a sense of love and concern for all the parties involved: the child itself, the parents, the family. They make that decision out of a sense of, I know it sounds odd to say love, but it's out of care and concern for everyone who would be affected as well as the family's long-term future for the next twenty or thirty years.

The souls of the parents would take that extra load back with them. Having felt they were forced to face that decision, they've had time in the human world to grieve for that child so that by the time the parents pass, their spiky energy from that event will have normalised back to a level playing field again.

The soul of the foetus that's been aborted would follow the same path as I've described for a miscarriage or a termination.

Is there ever a situation where a physical foetus dies without ever having had a soul?

No is the short answer, but it's a really logical question. If a foetus is going to die before full term, then the soul will make contact and take up residence, however briefly, before the death, irrespective of whether it's a miscarriage, stillbirth or even an abortion.

If the child is born and then dies very quickly after birth, it's the same situation. The soul will know and take up residence for whatever length of time it needed to make that connection.

It's as much about the needs of the soul as it is about the physical. So there's really nothing more to add except to say that, no, that situation doesn't ever arise.

What about multiple births – what happens to the soul or souls when non-identical twins or triplets are conceived?

For multiple births, however, many they are in number, the process is the same as for a single birth with the exception that multiple souls incarnate one into each embryo or foetus. The difference is that these souls have chosen to experience life as twins or triplets. When a pregnancy is recognised as being multiple births, a set of souls will put up their hands to incarnate together into that mother. They will usually wait until they can be certain that the foetuses will survive through to birth and beyond before they slip on board.

The extension to that is – what happens if one of the foetuses dies before or soon after birth?

It is the same process as when a single foetus dies. The soul will recognise that death is imminent and will slip out just before the end.

The difference though is that it knows that it is leaving its mate behind and it often leaves with much sadness because of that. During their time together in the womb, they have been mutual support for each other, taking comfort that the other is there sharing this journey with them. So there is usually a greater degree of sadness for these departing souls than when a single foetus, infant or child dies.

What happens with identical twins?

Good question! This happens when a single fertilised egg divides into two. So the question becomes – do these two embryos have two separate souls or has one soul split in line with the physical split? If so, how does a soul split?

The answer is that a single soul splits. It will have known before it chose this mother and pregnancy that identical twins were going to happen and the soul has chosen to have this split existence and experience. Each part-soul will then take up residence in each foetus or newborn at the time they chose which is in line with their soul plan.

So – how does a soul split?

What happens is that the energy bubble of each part-soul will have pretty much identical compositions. All the components will be shared almost equally between both halves of the soul. This is why identical twins display such similar and interconnected behaviour. They can often finish each other's conversations, know what the other is going to say before it is spoken and if for example, they are musical, they might even be able to spontaneously sing in perfect harmony. In other words, the split soul plus the split egg makes them carbon copies of each other in almost every sense.

That leads on to – what happens if one foetus dies in utero or as an infant or newborn?

That soul slips out just before death just like any other death but again with much sadness because it is leaving its other half behind, literally. It will await the return of the other part-soul even if that takes seventy or eighty years. After the second soul returns, they will reunite into the single soul that they started out as.

Does the surviving soul suffer throughout that life from the loss of its other half? If so how does that manifest in the human?

Initially irrespective of whether they are identical or not, the surviving twin will certainly feel that loss, more keenly in an identical twin because it is literally its other half. They had both planned to do this incarnation together, hand-in-hand, side-by-side, even if that's metaphoric, to be mutual support.

So right at the beginning it feels abandoned. Even though they understand that this is not a deliberate choice on the part of the departing soul, it still leaves its mark. It feels abandoned, lost and to start with, it struggles.

That can manifest, more so in identical twins, right through to adulthood. Sometimes the remaining twin, particularly when he/she gets to teenage-hood, will go in one of two directions. They will curl up and become hermit-like because they have no self-confidence. They will shrink within as their method of protection, or conversely (to use your phrase) they will go off the rails. They might get into extreme behaviour, drugs and alcohol to extreme degrees, all sorts of things that are going to hide or mask or avoid that loneliness and emptiness in the soul.

They will go through that introvert or extrovert teenage phase because there are also lots of other changes going on at that time. By the time they reach their twenties or mid-twenties, all that will have passed because they will have settled into their future lifestyle, whether that's work or family or whatever the norm will be for them.

I know those phases can manifest in lots of teenagers who are not twins, but if it is a twin, it is very likely to be caused by this sense of "I've still got to get through this on my own," with a sense of continuing underlying abandonment, aloneness, loneliness and feeling unsupported. But usually, by its mid-twenties, it will be back on track getting on with its life.

Do identical twins have a single soul plan or does each part-soul have its own?

That's a really good question. They have a single soul plan but once they incarnate, even as children growing up together, you can usually notice subtle differences in their behaviour or attitudes, sometimes more subtle than others. They do have a single soul plan even though the human traits might be slightly different in each.

To illustrate, let's say a soul has music as ten per cent of its soul. When the soul splits five per cent *more or less*, goes into each child. But it might be four and six per cent; it's not mathematically precisely equal. Therefore, as a teenager or adult, one twin might be a little less inclined to music than the other. They might show inclinations to different types of music because of that slight imbalance. If they both had exactly five per cent then what's the point of splitting? Let's come back to that.

Because they're not precision carbon-copies, they will display different behaviours and let's stick with music to illustrate. One might be interested in classical music and the other might prefer jazz. All the other components of their soul will be in slightly different proportions in each of them so that in adult life, one might become a politician who purports to be caring for his constituents. The other might become a careers adviser who is caring for his community of teenagers seeking careers advice. In their own way, they are both doing a caring role but it is manifesting in different ways. They are making different free-will choices because they're living independent adult lives. These free-will choices will mean that they make different decisions and behave differently. Nevertheless, in basic things they are effectively carbon copies of each other.

Which leads onto the question – why would a soul want to split when it has the one soul plan which means they are each trying to achieve the same goals in their individual lives? If they have come back to experience different things, why wouldn't they have separate soul plans?

Firstly, you can't have one soul trying to prepare two separate plans with different objectives; it's just not possible. Secondly, they only split at the point when they are getting ready to hop on board the two embryos or new-born infants. Up here it's only possible to have one soul plan for each soul.

Therefore, you have to ask – why wouldn't that soul remain complete and whole, and experience its soul plan in the normal fashion like everyone else?

These souls are almost always old souls with maturity and wisdom. They want or need to experience subtleties in whatever their strong qualities are. Let's continue with music. They will have had lives in the past in which music featured significantly. They might not be Chopin but they might have been a concert pianist or played in an orchestra, for example, earned their living from music I mean. This time they want to experience the different variations on that theme. If one is enjoying opera and other is listening to vocal jazz, these are both music and both are vocal but they are very different types of vocal music. They will go through life experiencing these subtle differences.

Most often as adults, identical twins remain enormously close to each other both emotionally and psychologically, even if they live hundreds of miles apart. So, what happens when they come back?

Both halves do their separate reviews and the part-souls then reunite to become the single soul it started out as. We don't have half-souls floating around up here. In that soul's energy bubble, it now has double the learnings and experiences from a single incarnation. They've had two incarnations in one. It now has both the classical vocal and the jazz vocal experiences blended back into its single bubble. If it had gone back as a single soul – any single soul can experience both opera and jazz, but together they have done it to a greater depth because it's become their passion and focus. A single soul would not have experienced the same intensity or depth or degree of learning. It gives them wider and deeper experiences.

Souls that do this are finessing and fine-tuning. They have had much experience with music over many incarnations and now they are just tweaking around the edges of their knowledge and experiences simply because, by this stage, there is very little left for them to learn about music.

A soul like that will be very unlikely to ever come back and do another incarnation in which music is significant because that energy component has been more-than-satisfied.

Why would a child be born to a family who can't feed it or support it?

The soul which comes into that situation chooses to do that. The parents have got pregnant willingly or unwittingly, it doesn't matter, and the soul has chosen that experience of poverty and starvation. Like every other possibility, it's wholly and solely a soul choice (pardon the pun!).

Chapter 3

THE EMBODIED SOUL

Where does an incarnate soul live?

Everywhere. All through. It was Deepak Chopra who identified that there is intelligence (I think was his word) in every cell in the body. Basically, the soul permeates every cell, every atom, and the space within and between the atoms. As you understand them, the structure of atoms is more space than hard matter. The soul is all in that space between the electrons and the other components. All through from your toenails to the tips of your hair.

Do souls vary in size? Might one soul take up more physical space in an adult human than another?

It's a bit hard to put physical measures on energy but souls only vary in size to a small extent. The soul of somebody who is really thin won't be half the size of the soul of somebody who is overweight.

So – if the soul is meant to fit an averagely proportioned human, what happens to an overweight person at one end of the spectrum, and an anorexic or bulimic person at the opposite end?

With the overweight or obese person, the soul will occupy the space where it needs to be to experience emotions and intellect and so on. Let's say, for instance, that today it wants to experience running. The soul will be in the legs and in the heart because it's pumping hard when you're running. There's not a lot for the soul to learn from sitting in all this slurry which is the excess fat. Can you imagine sitting in a pile of that… ugh! Horrible thought. Even though there's space, because even all this sludgy fat has atoms with emptiness inside and out, there's nothing much for the soul to learn from occupying that particular space.

Let's say that this person goes on a diet so that the fat slowly reduces. The soul would occupy that space for a little while to have that experience. Souls don't like the denseness of physicality never mind the thick, yukkiness of fat. The soul will occupy the bits where it can learn whatever it has come to experience. And that doesn't include sitting for weeks or months in buckets of fat.

At the other end of the spectrum of ultra-thin humans, the soul will start out in a normal-sized, if thinner, person. As the obsession continues and the weight comes off, the soul will squash in, to a certain extent. As the person gets to be so light-weight that the body is not functioning properly and they are approaching death, then the soul operates as it would for any death and takes its leave just before the physical end.

In between these extremes, the soul will come and go. Because the soul is a complete bubble the front-half of the bubble doesn't take up residence without the back-half. The whole soul would be in situ for a while but then take opportunities to come out but still be nearby and connected to the human.

The other part of this is that as very thin people get even thinner they have less energy. They do less physically but there is more mental activity as they get more and more stressed. The soul, which has chosen this anorexic person in order to experience the emotions associated with all this, is not going to go off and miss it. But if it gets to the point where it's a hard fit, it will flip out but still be close by.

Is the soul fixed in the same part of the body? Is it there all the time or does it move around? What is the trigger for that movement? Can bits of it move independently from the whole?

Let me answer the last bit first. The soul will move as a whole; it won't subdivide down. The bit that wants to experience running won't separate out from the whole. The whole soul would spread itself in the legs and the heart and the lungs for that experience.

So that goes on to say that it does move through the body in response to whatever activity is happening at any instant that it wishes to learn from. But it doesn't, therefore, follow that the brain or the arms are empty when it's running. Because it's energy and all fluid, which I say repeatedly I know, then the bulk of it will move down to the legs, but there will still be enough in the brain to experience the associated emotions and intellect, and in the arms which are pumping. But the bulk of it will be where the centre of this activity is.

Let's say you're in high school and you're trying to grapple with the intricacies of some maths problem. All the activity is in the logical left side of the brain because maths is pure logic. So the bulk of the soul will be in that part of the brain to have this experience. Now it won't all be there because on the right side of the brain there will be the emotional responses to this problem, either yippee, I've cracked it, or, I'm fed up with this because I can't do it. So there will be smaller amounts of the soul in the associated areas. But even when I'm sitting trying to do this maths, there will still be bits of the soul in the legs and the toes, even though they're passive. There is never a bit of the body that has no soul.

To illustrate, I've got in mind Casper the friendly ghost[2] who flows as a whole into different situations but adapts his shape accordingly. It's like that.

In a twenty-four-hour day, there are two distinct activity periods, namely waking and sleeping. What does a soul do during these two periods?

During its waking hours, a soul virtually mirrors whatever the human is doing. It's along for the ride so to speak, to have this myriad of daily experiences together with whatever bigger events sometimes happen.

However, at night time, the soul is free to escape, to zoom off into the night wherever it wants to go, free as a bird – well, even freer because it doesn't have to contend with the limitations of gravity. There are two things to say about this:

Firstly, its prime responsibility is to the human, its host, and it maintains contact which means that it's always alert to what the body is doing. If the human wakes up unexpectedly at three in the morning, the soul is *ping*, instantly back home. It will remain in residence until the next period of sleep irrespective of whether that's an hour later or the next night.

Secondly, that begs the question– why would it want to take off every night?

During sleep, the human body is physically on auto-pilot; it breathes, its blood circulates and all the other metabolic things happen without any conscious input from the brain, so there is nothing going on for the soul to experience. Because souls can struggle sometimes with

---

[2] Casper is a fictional character in an animated cartoon created in 1945.

this physical denseness, each night-time offers a respite, the chance for its own rest and recuperation. And this could be especially necessary if the human has had a really hard day.

Where does it go when it flies off?

It can go anywhere it chooses. Out to anywhere in the whole universe. It might want to meet up with old friends. Now if it does talk to other souls which are aware that our soul is doing an incarnation, then it is absolutely understood by everyone, that there can be no discussion whatsoever about any aspect of that incarnation. Every embodied soul must live its physical life without any external influence whatsoever from anyone upstairs.

Do dreams affect the soul?

That's a really interesting question. We need to look at dreams in the context of what they are.

Some dreams are just a regurgitation of activities that have happened during the day or very recently, stuff that's going around in the human's head. If you're worried about, say, a house that's being built opposite and it's noisy, then an intrusive activity like that might come back as a dream. The soul is not particularly affected by that. It might be aware but it might not even be in the body when dreams like that occur. Because you're just regurgitating what the soul has already experienced during the day, there's nothing to be gained by replaying it.

However, if a dream has a strong emotional content, then the soul is likely to be around to experience that especially when you wake up strongly remembering those emotions. So, the answer to the question is sometimes yes and sometimes no, depending on the nature of the dream.

Now the extension of that is – what about lucid dreams?

These are a very specific style of dream, which, on the whole, don't happen often. But when they do happen they're extremely intense and the soul certainly would want to have that experience, simply because it's seldom going to get the chance. So yes, it would definitely be around for that sort of dream.

Do these activities vary for, say, physically or mentally disabled people?

No. The physical or mental condition of the host makes no difference. All souls behave as I have described, regardless.

What is the purpose of dreams?

Dreams are like a safety valve. They exist to allow the emotions to escape in a harmless fashion. For instance, if a human is really worried about a friend who is ill, and let's say that by their nature they are a worrier, then that concern will just keep gnawing away at them. If it gnaws too much it can be physically detrimental; as we all know, stress and worry can cause illness. By having dreams around this ill person, it's a way for the emotions to be released to some extent. If it's a major concern this might take several nights after which this worry is not going to affect the physical to the same extent.

If you're angry about something, then you can vent verbally all you like at the people around you which doesn't help relationships and everyone gets upset. If you can release some of that anger through dreaming then you come back calmer and those around you don't suffer to the same extent either.

Do human milestones like marriage, the birth of a child, death of parents, significantly affect the soul?

Human milestones of any nature are sources for experiencing the greater extremes of emotions. A marriage, birth of children, a graduation, all manner of similar events will bring much joy and happiness, pride, maybe a sense of achievement. The death of anyone close will inevitably bring a torrent of grief and sadness and maybe some regrets. From the soul's point of view, these events enable it to experience these stronger and more immediate spikes of emotional energy which will probably only happen very occasionally during a human lifetime. It's likely that the soul has chosen this particular human in order to have these more extreme experiences too.

Which leads on to the next question – do only emotions affect the soul?

Well, yes and no. Physical activity is effectively the vehicle, the mechanism for triggering emotional reactions. Even basic choices like red socks or blue socks today will prompt some sort of response, albeit quite tiny in that instance. Bigger decisions like, will I stay home and work on my thesis or go for a drink with my mates, will generate larger and opposite reactions.

The 'no' part of the answer refers to the intellect. The soul will also experience intellectual activity. If for instance, you are struggling to make a big decision or you are grappling with some ethical dilemma, then a lot of mental activity is going on. This might continue for days or weeks even, all of which the soul experiences alongside the emotional reactions.

Where do those inspirational light-bulb moments come from?

Those *ah-ha* moments. Mostly they are a channel. Not in everybody. Some humans will have that knowledge tucked away in their brains and it will suddenly just pop up to the surface. Sometimes in people who are sensitive, it will be a channelled moment of *bing*. That's what they need to hear at this moment and we put it into their head. From a soul's perspective, it's no big deal.

How does a prolonged illness affect the soul? Does a mental illness affect the soul differently from a physical one?

Firstly, it is just another experience, albeit it can be extremely long. But we need to differentiate between a medical illness and the consequences of say a really bad accident resulting in a lot of physical damage. With the latter, once you get through the early trauma you will mostly recover. Even if it takes years of exercise and physio, the outcome will be good.

If the physical body is recovering slowly, the emotions which accompany that slow path will be up and down ("yippee, today I was able to walk that little bit further.") There will be all these high points of new achievements, so it will be a gradual positivity with periods of down especially at the beginning. If you were to draw a graph, it would slowly notch upwards until the recovery is either complete or as good as it's ever going to be. At that point, you have to settle into some acceptance of these new limitations but still be hugely grateful that you have come all this way from where you were at the time of the accident.

However, a medical condition which is debilitating but not life-threatening, like chronic fatigue, brings a range of different emotions, particularly if there is no end-point in sight, no cure or known means of getting out of it. Then the emotions range from despair and hopelessness, often to great depression, to sometimes slowly and gradually accepting and learning to live in the new, more limited lifestyle. Some people will never give up hope and keep battling away until they find a way to make life work for them again. So this brings a whole different range of emotions.

The extension of that is – what about a disease like cancer which can be long and protracted with remission periods but is still likely to be the cause of death?

It's going to be the same ups and downs of emotions. When you're in remission, it will be, "wow, let's get on with it because I don't know how long I've got," with lots of gratitude. Of course, heaps of hopelessness, fear, pain, why-me, especially in the beginning. If you're going through chemo, then it will be patience, gratitude for the support staff and the family who are looking after you. They're all vehicles for experiencing different combinations of emotions.

But the logical extension of this is – what about people who are on life-support machines?

Well, they are still physically functioning. Whether they're in a coma for a week or on long-term life support, the physical body is only operating to meet its minimum metabolic needs so the soul isn't learning or experiencing anything new.

So – what's happening to the soul when a human is in this situation?

Under these conditions, the soul will often be out but nearby because that's its job. It will likely come out, partly because there's nothing to learn or experience from this, but also because there's so much electrical energy (from electronic equipment) and unnatural intervention (like oxygen masks and catheters for instance) that the physical is not even functioning naturally. The soul will want to experience a little of that, but after that, there's nothing more to be learnt by staying in situ for weeks or months.

There might be mental activity of course and the soul will be alert to whether that's happening. It will be diminished but it might not be zero. There might be a lot of mental anguish going on which cannot be articulated. Under those conditions, the soul will be nearby, maybe up on the ceiling, because it's almost in limbo. What can it do? It's got no vehicle for learning.

Many people in the Western world spend years going to counselling to work through their issues which might be parental or sibling relationships, failed marriages, abuse. How does all this soul-searching affect the soul?

Pardon the pun! Counselling can cause the human to remember the issues in some depth which can bring pain or grief or anger or victim-mode or whatever emotions go with that. As you work through it sometimes you get the release and perhaps relief. Hopefully, you will get to a point of understanding and accepting that the other parties involved had different issues going on in their lives and perhaps didn't see it from your perspective when the problems occurred.

That's being very general around a very complex subject. It's yet another vehicle for experiencing quite deep, intense and prolonged emotions. What goes with that, of course, is trying to be logical. The analytical work and intelligence try to remember back to what happened and what was going on for the other people who were involved. So there's all this use of memory and analysis which are also different things for the soul to experience.

If in the end the issues are accepted or released and the need for counselling is finished, then the ensuing emotion is hopefully gratitude or relief that I don't have to keep on with this soul-searching, that I've solved it, that I can get on with my life. It's also a vehicle for those positive emotions at the end of the process.

Dementia is an increasing problem in the Western world today. What is happening to the soul under those conditions?

The soul has lost its vehicle for learning, that's what's happened. The poor soul is stuck. The poor human too, I don't diminish this. Dementia is a sad situation for the person, the family and the carers, there's no doubt about that, and it comes in many shapes and sizes. It can become advanced to the point that the human is only operating almost by instinct even though those instincts have now changed to, for instance, to paraphrase someone. If somebody says hello to you, you might say hello back without any understanding of what you are saying. Your instinct might now be to wander or to scream and yell, maybe out of frustration. But they have lost the ability to reason and think and remember.

That basically says that the soul has lost its vehicle for any sort of learning. In an older human who still has mental capacity in their later years, the soul can still learn and experience what life is like in a reduced physical state. These eighty- and ninety-year-olds still live a life albeit in reduced physical terms, but they will still have family and friends and phone calls and connections with other humans. So the soul is still able to learn and experience those things at the latter end of a human life.

With dementia the learning is non-existent; in some cases, it's backwards because it's not even remembering what it has learnt previously. In really severe cases where the human can't remember how to dress or feed themselves, then it's a retrograde situation and the soul is stuck.

Even under those conditions, the soul will never ever leave until the physical death has occurred. The soul might be flipping out more but always connected and nearby. It is never going to desert that human and again, it would only leave and fly off at night time when the human is asleep. It will still behave in the proper normal fashion but even if the soul is frustrated, well that's part of the deal at this stage.

That leads onto the question – did this soul know before it incarnated that this human was likely to develop dementia? The answer is probably sometimes yes and sometimes no.

Sometimes the soul will want that experience even though it's very hard to understand why you would want to spend years experiencing next-to-nothing as mental activity. That is the sad difficulty with dementia.

My sense is that increasingly souls did not put their hand up for this experience. It's happening in the human physical plane and is coming up on them even though they didn't set out with that goal. These souls just have to wait it out until the physical dies and do their best to cope during the day. They might come out and do more engaging activities at night time with other souls to compensate. Or they might be happy to be along for this quiet ride; not every soul needs to be actively engaged. If you were a soul in a couch potato you might have chosen that dementia experience because it will be similar to the rest of that life.

Anna wants children but discovers that she can't have them. She goes through life very distressed but she doesn't want to adopt. What happens to her soul?

Her soul will just go back with sadness and regret.

Because she didn't have the opportunity to live the life that she wanted?

Yes, that's possible. Some come in not wanting kids, and where that happens, it's as much about selecting that particular quality in the same way that you say, "I'm going to be a soldier," or "I'm not going to be a CEO." This is just another quality.

Where they wanted them and it hasn't happened, the parents, both usually, go back with disappointment, sadness, maybe regret, feeling unfulfilled, sometimes feeling victim. It's easy for me to say but if you don't want to feel victim, the one thing to do is try to adopt because then at least you have children and the experience of raising them, but that's a human choice. There are these emotional qualities that the parents and more particularly the mother would take back.

How and why do themes and emotions carry over from past lives? For instance, Anthea is obsessive about paper, any sort of paper. She knows now that she was a scribe in several past lives when paper was precious, but that's not the case in the 21st century. Why has this carried forward so strongly?

This can be for a few different reasons. Firstly, it might be a quality or theme that has not been fully met or satisfied in a past life or lives and needs to be experienced again this time around. That's the obvious reason.

However, it might also be coming through as a trigger for another related issue. In this example, you're right. Paper is everyday stuff in your world today and of itself, is not a concern. However, what is one of the prime uses for paper? Writing, of course, even if it's as much symbolic today with the advent of typing directly into computers. But what has she been doing for much of this life? Writing in its various forms. Paper is the link that carries forward from those past lives where she was a scribe in a monastery, to become the trigger which has led her down this path to this work that we're all doing now.

What's the view upstairs of gay folk?

The view up here is… the word tolerance comes to my head… we don't do judgement and there is certainly no concept that to be physically attracted to someone of the same sex is a problem. It's not a problem. It's a piece of human biological programming that has happened during foetal development and it's like saying you've got your wires crossed. That's a really simple analogy which doesn't carry any judgement about right or wrong. With the wires uncrossed you would be attracted to the opposite sex. With the wires crossed you become attracted to the same sex. It's never evident until the child is older.

The question then arises from a soul's perspective – does that soul know that it's going to come back and experience life attracted to the same sex. The answer is yes.

Firstly, as part of its plan, a soul will decide it wants to have the experience of living as a gay person – and there are extremes of life as gay people just as there are extremes of life in all sorts of ordinary folk. Then there has to be some sort of monitoring mechanism up here that says, "OK, Bronwyn over there is carrying a foetus who will end up gay because the physical wires have got crossed."

There is now this embryo available to a soul who wishes to experience a gay life. From there on, once that connection is made the rest follows in exactly the same way as any other soul. It will choose at what point it wishes to enter that foetus, and it will live through the life of that child, adult, until the end in exactly the same way as anyone else. The beginning is the only difference for gay folk.

What is happening with the soul of a person who feels that they have been born into the wrong gender body? Has there been some sort of mistake here?

My first sense is that the percentage of people, always adults, who have this really strong feeling and belief, has probably not changed much over the last several hundred years. The populations have grown so there will be more people like this, but in percentage terms, it's probably not much different.

What is different now is the greater social acceptance and much greater media coverage which means that communities are generally far more aware of this situation. In recent years surgery has become possible to rectify that if the person wishes to go down that radical and rather risky route, again a free-will choice. There's no judgement about whether they do or they don't. If you went back a hundred years, none of that surgery was possible, societies were more closed and such subjects were not commonly discussed.

What is going in with the soul in these folk, many of whom really struggle?

When the soul chose to incarnate into this human, it was aware that this would be a possibility in adult life. It knew that this human would become very unsettled and feel that they were in the wrong gender body. For its own reasons, this soul has chosen this foetus to have this experience, just like any other experience. It's a fairly radical and difficult experience and it takes a lot of courage until the human has developed enough confidence to enact or live or dress, or all of those, as the opposite gender. There can be a lot of mental and emotional issues and a lot of counselling to try and resolve it.

From the soul's perspective, it has usually chosen this because it has an issue about gender or sexuality. As I've said before, souls will always have more male qualities than female or vice versa. So, if it has a predominance on male traits but has been born into a female body, there's this potential for conflict. If those male qualities are really strong enough and come through, then this can lead to the female human thinking and feeling that she has been born into the wrong body.

People will cope and live with it by choosing lives where they can encompass those male qualities. They might work in a male-oriented world, or in your more egalitarian societies, she works in a male job. Maybe today she's a truck driver whereas fifty years ago it would have been almost impossible for a woman to work in that capacity.

Others will say that they absolutely don't want to be female and insist on being male. They will dress as a male, only have men friends, only have male social activities like going to the pub with men, right through to undergoing sex reassignment surgery. It is not black-and-white; it's obviously a graduation between these two extremes. But wherever you are on that spectrum, the whole thing is a huge, huge issue.

Coming back down the spectrum from having surgery, the person might be dressing and living that male life. You use the term cross-dressing for these folk. If a soul chooses a human who is likely to only become a cross-dresser in adult life, is that the same sort of thing or is something different going on with those souls?

No, it is the same thing and again they have chosen to have this experience. Cross-dressers are only a step along that spectrum and there are variations within that category. Some are happy being occasional cross-dressers; others are happy working in that capacity. To illustrate I have the film *Priscilla, Queen of the Desert* in mind where the men were portrayed as very happily working as extremely obvious cross-dressers.

A soul will choose this life in the same way that it chooses any other quality and it might choose this lifestyle just once to satisfy this need. I know your societies still find it odd but from the soul's perspective, there is nothing bad or wrong about it.

Does a soul know before it incarnates that it will have a long or short life or if that life will include major trauma or be totally peaceful?

In the sense that it has planned this upcoming life around its needs for learning, then yes it does. However, what it never has any control over is human free-will. Let's say a soul planned to have a long and peaceful life. But one night the young student who is hosting this soul gets very drunk and drives home. He has a nasty accident resulting in very serious injuries which take him several years to recover from. These two free-will choices, to get drunk and then to drive, have resulted in a long period of upsetting and traumatic existence. If the car accident had resulted in his death, well, suddenly it has become a very short life.

What is the purpose of free-will when it can be counter-productive to meeting the goals set in a soul plan?

The purpose of free-will was to give choices to any human which meant you could choose the experiences you wanted to have. If you incarnated without free-will you would be like an animal on a pre-programmed loop. If you had come to do music, for instance, you would just plod through it in a mindless fashion without thinking about what options there were within that sphere. You wouldn't differentiate between say learning classical violin or playing drums in a rock band. So the whole point was to give the experience of choice.

Now choice always encompasses options which can be beneficial or detrimental to yourself, those around you or, in exceptional cases, to the world around you. If you chose to become the President of the United States, then that choice affects all the millions of people in that country. If you chose to become Hitler then his choice to move into that position of power ended up affecting all the folk who died in the Holocaust.

It's about giving the soul the experience of using the intellect... because otherwise why do you need an intellect? Animals don't have an intellect in the way humans do; they live on auto-pilot. It's dark; we sleep. But humans don't do that. It's dark; I can go out to dinner or I can watch TV or I can go to bed. The intellect gives humans the ability to think about different choices which in turn, provides a wider range of possibilities for experiences.

Where do judgements fit in because they are also free-will choices?

Judgements are human and only human. Every human, whether he's Chinese, an Eskimo, a Peruvian Indian, anyone, even if he's outside the Western concept of education, can make judgements.

You could argue that the more information that you have the better able you are to form a judgement. For instance, you know that your scientific history says that at one time we believed that the world was flat but now science has shown that the world is round. These days, many hundreds of years later, you have knowledge of both, so you are able to form a judgement about which of those views you believe.

If today you are a tribesman deep in the Amazonian jungle who has only known his own culture which, by Western definition is not educated, he will still have the ability to make judgements about, for instance, whether nature is changing. He will have enough knowledge, as distinct from information, to ask whether the climate has been different this year and will this affect his crops or animals differently.

Judgements are not just confined to a basis of education. They are a function of prior experience, and then remembering and learning from those events. The Amazonian tribesman will know that by this time in previous years his crops were so high but this year they're not. So he can make a judgement that something has changed.

I'm trying to differentiate between a society which is based on formal education, and people still living in their own ethnic cultures, untouched by Western-based society. Their knowledge and learning of their own culture, which will largely be based on nature, will still enable them to make these judgements based on remembering prior experiences.

Judgements were designed for survival, to enable this tribesman to say, "Oh dear, my crops are not as they should be at this point in the season. Can I, and what do I need to do to rectify that?" so that he will survive into the future. In Western society, we still make judgements to survive. "Do I step in front of this oncoming car and get knocked over or not?" Those are practical, survival-type judgements which still almost serve the original purpose for which they were designed.

Then you get into the judgements of good and bad, positive and negative, right and wrong. Making a judgement about whether a situation is good or bad for you as an individual, you could argue is about survival. To illustrate, you meet a new person and you quite like this person, but as you get to know them you see bits that you're not so comfortable with. Eventually, you have to make a judgement, which leads to a decision, about whether you wish to spend more time with them. If you judge, not that they are a bad person, but from your perspective, their influence is not going to be helpful or beneficial – and that is you making that judgment – then you might choose not to pursue that relationship. That's about emotional self-protection and survival at the basic level.

You can then take that up to a societal level if you like. To illustrate:

> Countries like the European nations, just for example, will make a judgement that the way ISIS is behaving is bad and has been demonstrated to be damaging to folk in Paris and Brussels recently[3]. At a societal level, the governments will make a judgment that this is detrimental and then use that judgement to make a decision about what to do to protect their citizens.

Judgements should be used to rationalise a situation and then use that analysis to come to a decision about the next step or future actions. That really was the purpose of judgements.

Can you tell us about instinct and intuition? What is the difference? How do they affect the human soul?

---

[3] The Paris bombings in November 2015 and Brussels bombings in March 2016 were carried out by ISIS.

Instinct is largely inbred through the genes; intuition is a subconsciously learned response. Animals follow their instincts. All of that is pre-programmed and by that I mean those instincts come from their parents through the genes. Humans are the same. If you see a bus steaming towards you as you step out onto the road, your survival instinct will kick in – and interestingly Jung and Freud had some of that right about survival instincts – and you jump back out of the way. Basic instincts are survival, procreation, sleeping and eating.

Intuition, however, comes from the brain and often it comes unknowingly from the soul. To illustrate:

> Anthea was walking down a busy main street in New York with a handbag hanging over her shoulder. Unbeknownst to her, a pickpocket was just behind her trying his best to get into the handbag. Some intuition suddenly made her become alert. She turned around to see a young man standing about two inches away with his hands above his head as if to say, "I'm nowhere near your bag, lady." But both instinctively and intuitively she knew. So her judgement kicked in and said, "I don't think I should have this bag over my shoulder." She made a decision to move it to the front where nobody could get at it without her seeing them.

That's actually a good example of the instinct and intuition leading to a judgement which leads on to a decision which then transforms into an action. In this instance it was her intuitively sensing, it's a sixth sense really, that said something's not right. Then you're alert and you respond and whether that's an instinctive or a logical response depends on the circumstances. Intuition is inbuilt but it needs a sixth-sense stimulus or catalyst to kick it into action. People often say that they feel a reaction in their stomach or abdomen.

Coming back to the soul, instinct is nothing to do with the soul, but intuition is largely from the soul and often, not always, from the soul's experiences in past lives which are the root source of intuition. It's collective wisdom from past lives which lie dormant but if a situation requires it and there is a catalyst, it will kick into action.

What is the role of the ego? How does it affect the soul?

In the original design for humankind, it was never intended that there would be an ego in the way that you understand that word today. It was never intended in the 'I am' sense, eg I am better, I am more important. The original plan was that humankind would be community-focused which leaves no need for an ego. In that situation, my focus is that I am looking after my family and I'm helping my neighbours if there's a need. If my neighbour asks for help I will always do my best to give that assistance. If that request comes when there is a conflict with my family needs, then I will do my best to accommodate both but if I can't, then my neighbour would always understand that my family will come first for me as his would for him.

Under that model, there's no need for an 'I am' ego. Nobody is better than anyone else. Once you get a religious dimension in your community, there are elders, but in our idealistic model, they were there to offer guidance. They were not there to say, "I am an elder, therefore, I am bigger and better." That was never the plan.

These days virtually the whole of humanity is a million miles from that ideal. Somewhere along the line, the ego evolved because what is tied up with ego is competition. If you are running a competitive race, then every person in that race has an ego that says, "I want to win because I need to win because my ego says that I am the best or I want to be the best."

If you are living in a mutually-supportive community there is no need for competition even if you're selling your goods in a marketplace where there might be several stalls selling similar goods. If we go back thousands of years, we were selling goods because we all needed to raise money to support the family. All merchants understood that some customers would like merchant A's goods and others would prefer merchant B, and that was fine. If times were tough they would even help each other.

Today shops and market stalls are competitive but sometimes this is more about ego than competition. Up here we accept that it is now part of virtually every human culture. There might be a few ethnic cultures who are still living without it but they are such a tiny minority on your earth-plane that they're not going to have any global effect.

From the soul's perspective, what is the purpose behind out-of-body experiences (OBEs) particularly when it can fly off every night anyway? What about astral travel?

Good question. OBEs tend to only occur when the human is in some sort of trance or dream-like state. They do not occur when you are standing on the high street trying to get a taxi, ie when your consciousness is fully engaged. They occur in situations which are similar to sleep and they often occur at night-time when the physical is asleep.

Then you have to ask – what's the difference between a soul flying off normally at night and an OBE?

From the soul's perspective, there is no difference except that after an OBE the human recalls what has happened. The human consciousness connects enough with the soul that when the soul flies off somewhere, the next day the human can say that I had an OBE or I astral-travelled last night.

That then begs the question – what is the difference between an OBE and astral travel?

With an OBE the soul flips out for a short period and then flips back and the human will consciously remember that. Astral travel is an extension of that when the soul goes off for hours and hours while the human is asleep. It's the same process for the soul but this human has developed the ability to consciously remember and recall that journey when he wakes up.

The body was never designed for humans to remember that. During sleep, the whole body, including the consciousness, is working on metabolic auto-pilot which is meant to give the consciousness as well as the physical a chance to rest. The whole point of the soul flipping out at night is to provide its own rest and recovery. I know that people will train themselves to be able to do this, and of course, it's a human free-will choice but it can come at a cost to the physical. Curiosity will motivate this and if you are into the esoteric world, there are often drivers to try and learn this. If the human found that they became tired or confused afterwards, hopefully, they would stop doing it.

Do flying dreams reflect an astral-travel journey?

Good question. Flying dreams are in between not remembering at all and this OBE/astral-travel remembering. For reasons only known to the soul, this will manifest as a flying dream. The dream is not always literal about flying off through the blackness to Sirius for example; it's often about flying within your physical world somewhere. It's mainly symbolic and is usually, but not always, indicative that the soul has gone off and it wants you to know that.

I can't give you an answer as to why; the reasons are up to the soul and it's going to be individual each time. The progression is from no-remembrance to flying dreams to a short memory recall after an OBE flip to a long astral travel journey with remembrance, at the other end of that spectrum.

From a soul's perspective, what is the purpose behind a near-death experience (NDE)?

An NDE will occur when there has been either some major trauma to the body or a serious illness which is slowly getting worse to the point where the physical will sort of want a rest – it's a funny word. The soul will know through that period of decline that a death event is very likely. Like the permanent death situation, the soul will flip out but be close by and attached before this NDE happens.

Before the NDE actually happens there is still the possibility that it won't occur, but for whatever reason, the physical dies in the clinical, technical sense. The soul has already flipped out, completely understanding what's happening, totally connected and around still. That NDE might last seconds or minutes.

The logical extension is when someone goes into a coma and comes back, but in either case, the duration is variable. The soul will know when the physical comes back to life and will instantly flip back in. From then on the soul will continue on with that human's life even if that is only short.

This gives the soul the opportunity to experience what it's like to flip out at the end of the physical. You then have to say – why would the soul want what is effectively a practice run?

Well, it hasn't chosen this human to have this experience; it has pretty much come from the physical. The human might have had a heart attack or a dreadful car accident or perhaps an asthma attack which results in the physical being debilitated to the point that it stops. So the soul is only reacting to the situation that the physical creating.

Now you have to ask why – would the physical chose to do this?

Leaving aside the cardiac arrest where you get intervention in the form of the shock treatment to revive the heart, if it's something like an asthma attack or an accident, something in the physical will say, "I don't wish to die at this point; I want to keep living," and this will kick-start the physical.

Then you have to ask – what has been that trigger for the physical to make that choice because it's still a choice.

That will largely be the soul saying, "it's not yet time." The human might recall going to see the light; often they recall seeing friends and family who are saying, "much as we'd love to have you back, it's not yet time and you have to return."

That in part is the soul going off and seeing all that, and in part, it might be the soul itself saying that it's not time yet. With a soldier who is shot during war, his soul knows that it's not time but the physical has gone, its time cut short prematurely. With an NDE there's almost a choice. With these visions and messages that the human often recalls later, the soul is proactively trying to kick-start the physical again. So, it's a combination of this together with timely medical intervention. NDEs by definition always live; they never chose to die.

Why would a soul want to experience extreme high-risk activities like skydiving or motor racing?

Why does it want to experience anything? Some souls have a high element of risk in their soul bubble's energy components so they relish skydiving or surfing or whatever. It might also be that it's had a previous life or lives, which have been fairly sedentary, gentle and low-risk and it wants to experience the opposite. This soul's energy bubble would contain an average level of risk but when an opportunity arises it chooses to have that balancing experience.

What is a karmic group?

A karmic group of humans is a cluster of souls who, during their independent planning processes, have agreed collectively to come back together. For two reasons: to advance the objectives in their individual soul plans by working together and having mutual support, and, to become a cohesive adult human force in whatever their chosen career and paths are for this incarnation.

Siblings are often a karmic group – and that group can be as small as two or three. Not always but when you find siblings who are really close to each other, who spend a lot of time together even as adult families, they can be karmic groups. To illustrate:

> I've got Winston Churchill and his war cabinet in mind. They all worked together endlessly through the Second World War, for the same goal and purpose. Some of the aristocracy, who were in the war cabinet could have been a karmic group who had come back together with the shared purpose of supporting and guiding their nation through that war-torn period.

Would members of a karmic group have experienced past lives together? How do they choose the other members of their group?

Yes, they have often shared past lives but not always. Three answers really.

When there have been shared past lives, they are sometimes carrying forward collective unfinished business. They might have set some group objectives to meet, collectively as well for each of their soul plans, but they might not have achieved that. So they might come back again as a karmic group to have another go at trying to meet those particular goals.

They may not have had past lives together, and Ben comes to mind here. As you will read, he has picked his group of school friends because they are all souls – and a karmic group – who came in with a collective, common goal of using technology for some good for humanity. At the planning stage, they would have discussed trying to form a group of mates so they could collectively support each other to achieve their common goal.

The third reason is that they could also have shared past lives but this time they choose to come back because in that past life they were successful in achieving their common goal. In this life, they might now all be fascinated by the same interests and have the same sort of goal. So they agree that because they all worked well together last time, then let's have another go at working together again this time. I'm not saying that this is necessarily the case with Ben and his mates.

How does the human physical form affect the soul?

Souls up here will decide whether they want to incarnate into a human earthly life or whether they want to experience an existence on another galaxy or star system somewhere else. Any soul wanting an earthly incarnation can only choose a human simply because animals don't have souls.

Just to illustrate, it can choose a poverty-stricken Russian doing it hard in the backwaters of Siberia, it can be Donald Trump with his millions lauding it over America, it might be a Maasai warrior or anything else in between. There is a multitude of choices within the human context to give a soul very different experiences and it is a significant part of its soul plan to decide which part of humanity it chooses.

This might sound like a daft question but what exactly is love? I ask because that word is used in all sorts of contexts including things like 'love is the answer' and 'love is all.'

The movie *Love Actually* was all about love in all its different forms. It was a wonderful expression of how love manifests. Anyway, that doesn't answer the question.

At the basic level, love is a quality that is imbued in every soul's energy bubble just like intelligence or sense of humour or anything else. Love can come in different forms: parental love, parent to child, sibling love, really close friends, grandparent to grandchild which can be really strong, romantic love, longstanding relationships where we are totally comfortable with sharing our lives after forty years of happy marriage. There's huge variation.

Then the question becomes – are all those variants separate components in the soul's energy bubble or does this component called love bend and fluctuate according to the situation? I think the answer is more likely the latter.

When a baby is born its first contact is going to be the parents, particularly the mother. It will bond with the mother and right from the beginning that love component in its energy bubble will be a connection, not love in a pro-active sense but a bonding, with Mum, and as time goes on, with Dad.

As the baby becomes a toddler it will come to recognise that there are siblings who will play and interact with it, so it will develop a bonding connection with them particularly if they are relatively close in age. As it grows it will go to school and comes to understand that there are other humans outside this small group that you call a family. It will interact with them particularly these days when toddlers go to playgroups and daycare where they spend a lot of time interacting with other youngsters.

Around the age of three or four, it will learn that there are some humans of its own age group that it likes or doesn't like. That's the first thing – like and love are all tied in together, and love has its opposite of not liking. So it will learn fairly early on that I don't like this child with the black hair at daycare. From that, it will learn to avoid this child.

As it goes through school it will become more rational about liking and loving. With a bit of luck, it will also become discerning as well particularly, sadly, in Western societies where there are much greater risks for personal safety than there ever used to be, things like abductions and paedophiles and all those horrid things that never used to happen. So hopefully the parents will teach it and it will learn some discernment which will then filter through to, "do I want to like you?" or "is it safe to like you?" which are also about personal safety as well as love.

Then we go through the teenage years where the hormones kick in. It's the start of adult types of love and by that, I mean more than just sex or lust. To illustrate:

> A small group of really close school friends has such a strong bond between them; they are such a strong mutual support team. They spend most of every day with each other; if they've got a school problem they will ring or email each other. There is a huge bond of love between them which will carry them through, often for their whole lives.

That's like close-mates 'love' and it is a form of love. I know blokes especially would never express it that way, but that's what it is. Plenty of adults have close friends who they first met at the age of five or seven; that's another form of love. Romantic love comes in a variety of forms from that first attraction right through to long-lasting happy marriages – and gay or straight, it makes no difference.

Lust is not necessarily an expression of love although it was originally designed that the sexual would be part of a love relationship, just as going to the supermarket together or raising the children together is part of that. Sex would be part of a grander, overarching, deep, long-lasting love which can also manifest in all sorts of adult ways including mutual support, and care when somebody is ill.

As teenagers reach adulthood and very often through their twenties, they will then meet the person – gay or straight, again no matter – that they will choose to spend the rest of their lives with. The reason for that is that in straight relationships, that's the best time for the woman to have the children. Physically she is at peak fertility; she is best able to cope with the rigours of birth and subsequently raising the children. That's the reason for trying to find your long-term mate early on. I know these days that marriages don't last and divorcees will find new partners, but these are different manifestations of adult love.

Anthea sometimes drives past a tatty old van which has 'love is the answer' painted on the back, and in a way that is absolutely right. It's just so screamingly obvious to me that love *is* the answer and Jesus' message of 'love thy neighbour' was being espoused thousands of years ago. It is the answer and it's not new.

So what is happening from the soul's point of view? The love component in the soul's energy bubble will evolve as the human grows and has the opportunity to experience these different sorts of love. The component will blend and meld and flow and change and react because it's not reacting in isolation from the rest of the bubble's components. To illustrate:

> You're at a party meeting a new person; your consciousness is summing up this person; your visualness is saying, "Yes, I think he looks quite nice. He's nicely dressed and he speaks quite well so he's clearly got a brain." You're doing this analysis. If you spend enough time with this person, the love component in your soul will respond to the intellect's input and say and "Yes, I do quite like the look of this person and maybe I would like to have coffee with him next week."

Love in the soul is not operating in isolation.

The same thing is happening in reverse when you meet someone where you say, "ah, I'm not sure about this person." In that case, the intellect is raising a red flag and the unlike part of the love component will kick in and say, "I think you should be careful here." Intuition will flag up and say, "I'm not really sure about this." So you can see how these soul bubble components all work together.

The different phases of human development are opportunities for that love component to experience love in all these different ways.

Chapter 4
THE SOUL AT AND BEFORE DEATH

What happens to the soul at the point of death?

Under conditions of a normal death, the majority of which will be from old age, wear and tear, the soul will always know that the end of the physical is imminent. The soul will drift out of the physical and remain nearby before the actual end. You may have heard stories about the soul floating on the ceiling looking down on the body; that's pretty much what it does. It will always stay there until the body physically stops functioning. That is absolutely clear, categorically.

Sometimes it will hang around a bit. Sometimes it will be quite sad because it's had a nice journey with this human. Because it's really enjoyed the experience it doesn't quite want to leave even though it knows it has to. It will stay for as long as it chooses.

There's often a sense of sadness because every soul knows that an incarnation is finite and will end. Sometimes it will float up gradually looking back but still maintaining that connection.

If it's had a bad experience with this human or not as satisfactory as it had hoped, it might just be up and out. Sometimes it will whoosh off because it's had enough. There's every possibility in between as well of course.

I know you have stories about the soul being led to the light with lots of family and friends waiting to meet and welcome it and, depending on its circumstances; some of our angelic realms might be there to greet it as well. For a normal death from old age, that's still a good picture of what happens. This group of genuine welcomers are really pleased to see that soul back again, all really wanting to metaphorically give it a big hug and how fantastic it's back and really lovely stuff like that. Lots and lots of love in that welcome, huge amounts of love on the whole.

Every single soul that returns from a life goes through the same process. Absolutely everyone. That encompasses murderers, paedophiles, parents, teachers, nurses, gay folk and infants. It has as much rest and recovery as it needs, it does a review of the life just ended and the outcome from that will guide it towards whatever it is going to do next and when.

If a soul feels tired and has done a lot of what it wanted to do and it just wants to stop, is there any reason why it should carry on?

The timing for when a soul chooses to leave is totally at the soul's discretion. Up here we can't ever say an individual soul is going to leave on 27 February next year, for example. It's not within our remit or our control and it's not our prerogative to tell a soul when to come back. It's always up to the soul to finally make the decision that they want to return and that this is now the right time.

For every single soul on this planet, the soul is the single and only and whole decider of when it chooses to leave the physical. If the soul feels it has done enough, it might feel the physical is getting too hard, it might feel I've got nothing left I need to do. It might feel I have set my affairs in order and been a responsible person. If it feels there's no point any longer – and that usually summarises it – then it's totally at the soul's discretion and choice and decision, whether it's today, tomorrow or next week.

It's also the soul's choice, discretion and decision whether you jump under a bus, whether you lie quietly in bed or whether you take an overdose. It is totally, utterly, one hundred and ten per cent that soul's choice. It is a collective decision between the physical, the soul, the brain and the emotional you; they've all got a view. Nobody ever tells you… your friends might tell you, but that's out of care and love, and not wanting to see you physically go, but that's a separate issue.

Can people who have died gently and quietly not realise that they have died?

Yes, definitely. Because the transition is so gentle and the body is in a low, depleted state by that stage – it's on the verge of stopping altogether – so there's no impetus to contrast with this overall gentle, almost blissful state to make it aware of passing. It just lifts out without realising.

After you have died and your soul passes, is there any chance that any of its components can be lost?

No – it's like a bubble that can't burst. That's a good way of illustrating it. It doesn't change when it's incarnate. The bits you need to activate and interact within human form come to the fore. The ones that are not in your soul plan for this life, just recede and sit it out in the back seat, along for the ride so to speak.

What about death through an illness like cancer?

Pretty much the same process at the point of death. The difference is that the soul has known for a long time that this illness is going to be the cause of death. Often the human will have been given guidelines about the amount of time that's left and the soul will have an idea of its own volition anyway. Towards the end, the soul will just make the most of that remaining time because even a diminishing physical body is still an experience for the soul to go through. It will be around in the normal fashion all the time for that last lingering encounter and once the point of death approaches it will go back as I just described.

Many people experience horrendously traumatic events in their lives. What happens to their souls?

I keep thinking of all those souls who died in World War I under such awful conditions – totally unnecessarily but we're not going down that path – and all of them came flooding back here so quickly for that whole period. The Second World War too. Bang, bang, bang, bang, bang. All the time, every day. Those poor, poor souls. They didn't know what had happened to them.

It's worth differentiating between a soul that has had a traumatic experience like the loss of a child or a partner during its life but then continued on, from a soul whose life has ended traumatically like having a head chopped off or being shot in wartime or the victims in Hiroshima. In all those cases the soul was suddenly and unexpectedly catapulted out of the body.

In energy terms, the difference is this: when a child dies the parents have human time to grieve and come to terms with it. If you were to draw a graph of that experience, when the traumatic event happens the energy graph goes whoosh downwards. It instantly spikes and stays down within the parents for ages and ages. But as the grieving progresses and they slowly adjust, that energy spike will slowly pick up. By the time they die, they carry the energy of that experience with them but it has settled down into being part of their experience of that whole life albeit a very spiky, horrid piece of that life.

They don't come back traumatised in the same way as the poor soldier who has been shot in the back on the beach and landed face down in the water and suffocated. His soul is just traumatised because the physical has stopped instantly. In an experience like the death of a child, the physical continues in the parents and gives support and nourishment to the soul to overcome the emotion attached to this. But the soul of the soldier just goes whoosh out and upwards carrying the instant maximum emotional trauma back with him. That's the difference.

Is it true that an unexpected traumatic death will result in an instant return?

Going back to my poor soldier, his soul will be met up here by folk who will give it extra-large doses of love and support. Now because it needs a much longer-than-usual period for rest and recovery, it's not in a position to instantly reincarnate. So the short answer is, extremely unlikely.

There is a view that if you commit suicide you'll go to hell. Alternatively, there's another view that you will return immediately to do another life as a punishment? What is the view upstairs about that?

A load of rubbish! I don't want to go anywhere near the concept of hell. It's not what we're talking about. With suicide, the concept of coming back as a punishment is a valid question.

Irrespective of whether suicide is the cause of death, there is no concept whatsoever of ever having to reincarnate as a punishment. That is nonsensical – as well because a punishment presumes a judgement and we don't judge. There *is* no judgement, therefore there's no blame, there's no 'it's your fault' or 'you did it wrong.' There's none of that. Therefore, there's no concept of punishment. So the concept of coming back as a punishment for suicide or anything else is non-existent.

What happens after a suicide returns?

A soul who suicides returns upstairs instantly just like anyone who's died, but it comes back with the extra dimension of intent. It intended to come back. The soldier who has been shot has died without that conscious intent. I know he knew that the risk of death was higher but he didn't consciously set out to die. Or a car crash, that's a better example. You're driving along and you have a car crash then you're killed and your soul is catapulted out of your body. There was never any intent to die at that instant.

Conversely, suicides intend and this intent is carried back with them as an extra energy component in their soul. Given that the vast majority of souls return from old age and natural death, suicides are a tiny minority of all the returning souls. There are accidents and in wartime, there is a bigger influx of souls returning unexpectedly but in peacetime, suicides are a tiny, tiny percentage.

Virtually every suicide happens because the human can no longer cope with his physical life and circumstances. He finally decides this is the only way out. He's often hugely psychologically depressed, feels trapped and that there's no other escape. It's often a vicious cycle. Depression can go round and down in ever-deepening cycles so they can also come back with this extra emotional load of depression. Not always guilt. Some feel that they have… not been forced to it (that's the wrong word) rather that they had no choice. (That's a better phrase). They come back with this extra energy, sometimes the depression, the guilt and this intent to end their own life.

All that has to be dealt with in terms of Firstly, their rest and recovery and support phase, and then it's an extra dimension to be assessed in the review.

Everything else about what happens once they're back here is the same as anyone else. Let's say they suicided at the age of thirty. They might have had twenty-five years of good life, so there's all that to assess in the usual way. Then there's been this last five years that got so bad that it ended up in suicide to be assessed as well. A huge extra load as to why and all the things that led up to it.

Is euthanasia the same situation?

Euthanasia is a half-way house. Euthanasia virtually always happens when the human knows that their situation is going to get worse – and it's virtually always physical deterioration – without any chance of ever getting out of that downward spiral. In caring terms, this will cause a lot of upset, grief and physical load on their family and partners, and as they deteriorate so that load gets greater. Sometimes there's not the money to afford care which is an extra emotional burden. You can't generalise of course but usually, they would have decided in their own minds that this is the route they want to choose before they talk with the partner or family. By definition, you have to have somebody to help you, particularly if, for instance, you are physically paralysed. You can't do it by yourself. That's without getting into the legalities – an absolute nightmare, absolute lunacy but I'm not getting into that.

There's an energy of intent which comes back but it's not as strong as suicide. Like suicide, it is also pre-meditated and considered but euthanasia folk are usually not so depressed and are not guilt-ridden in the same way. They know they do it with the support and love of their family and often they have to do it with the physical support of those around them. If you are going to do it in a country where it's legal, the family has to get you there and all the arrangements have to be made for that to happen.

It's often done out of a sense of love and not wanting to be a burden on the family, as much as not being able to face the life that's left. There's too much love between the partners and in the family that they want to remove this huge overwhelming, ever-growing load of care and often financial drain. They just see this as the only way out.

They come back with relief, absolute relief. The physical enactment of suicide will be fairly quick, whereas with euthanasia, they think about it, they talk about it, they have to plan it, they have to manage it, and they have to get there. There's all this time leading up to it so in a way, it's a bit like grieving in that the emotional load is spread. It's not a big spike in emotional energy like suicide. When they come back, alongside the relief there's much, much sadness that they've had to do it this way. Usually no regret. Relief that they've been able to release the family to get on with their own lives, with love. Huge love in this process.

That soul will come back with extra elements because it's still got all its earlier life which was good, marrying, having children and whatever it's done. All that has to be reviewed in the standard way but it also has the extra elements of these qualities to be assessed as well. Sometimes it needs above-average support and rest when it first arrives back. Sometimes not so because physically it's often been bedridden for a long time but it does need that extra emotional support which is not as drastic and or radical as the suicides.

But on the other side, there is the question of whether the soul is missing out on this last bit of learning when euthanasia ends a life before its natural end. Well, that, in fact, is the case. Then you might ask – is it the soul's choice or is it a human choice?

Well... how long is a piece of string? Under human conditions like this, the free-will is going to kick in pretty much every time because the human just can't face what's left. By the time you're in that situation, you already know that you're in a bad way physically, so you're not thinking, "perhaps I'd better hang around because my soul still needs to learn." Those people mostly won't even be aware that the soul needs to learn, that's the first thing. Secondly, it's all about the human situation, the family and financial situation, the whole load of what's involved in going through to the end, is the dominant factor in making that choice.

What is the view upstairs about murder and what happens to the soul of the murdered person?

In terms of soul behaviour, the victim is virtually in the same situation as the poor soldier I keep talking about. Murder is unexpected on the part of the victim and the soul is usually just catapulted out at the instant that the physical body stops functioning. In soul terms, it's effectively the same as any unexpected traumatic death. Murder is just another human means of inflicting an unexpected traumatic ending.

From the point of view of the murderer, which I know leads onto the next question…

What happens to the soul of the murderer?

And the next question after that is about socially-inappropriate behaviours, rapists, paedophiles, etc.

What's the view about those and are their souls treated any differently when they return?

The first thing to say is that there is no way anybody up here condones or endorses or supports any of these utterly extreme and barbaric anti-social behaviours. But it's up to humans to run their world and live their lives through human choice. We're not able and it's not our place to judge or interfere. We can't. We have no mechanism for interfering, even if we wanted to.

All those anti-social behaviours tie in together really. Humans who engage in extreme socially-inappropriate activities – murderers, paedophiles, rapists, child abusers, not just physical abuse, emotional abuse I would put in there as well. You can think of lots of situations. The first question is – why do they do this in the first place? And what on earth is going on with those souls in a murderer or rapist, for heaven's sake?

Let me explain. Often a person who is likely to exhibit these behaviours will have had feelings and inclinations in this direction in late teens or young adulthood, even if they do not become publicly obvious until later in life. Young adults might not physically have the strength or the means to do it, by which I mean the axe or whatever ghastly thing he's going to do. He might not have had the opportunity. For the rape or murder or the paedophilia, the situation has to be set up in order to create the opportunity to kill or rape. You can't just turn up at a shop and pick a victim. It takes adult maturity and self-confidence as much as these dark thoughts and needs – because they are needs in a very perverse way – for that person to actually enact that piece of behaviour.

The first thing is, and you can't generalise, that for people who are seriously intent on this sort of behaviour, it will be long-standing in their psyche. It won't just suddenly pop up one day and say, "oh, I think I'll go and murder someone."

The soul knew this at the beginning and, in the same way, as a soul chooses to be a carer or a teacher or whatever else, these souls have chosen to join a human who is going to exhibit extreme behaviour of an anti-social nature.

Now you would have to say – why would somebody want to experience that?

Here's one example that just popped into my head. Let's say a soul chooses to experience being a murderer and when that life ends by whatever fashion, he goes back and reviews it. In time he comes back again saying, "I'm going to be an author. I'm going to write about murders," because he can do that from first-hand experience. That may not be a good example but it's one that's plausible.

At the end of that life, the soul of the murderer or the rapist or the paedophile comes back. It goes through the same process of rest and recovery and does the review, but the review is going to take a very different direction. Its content is going to be skewed towards these barbaric behaviours and there's going to be a lot of, pardon the pun, soul-searching as to why it did what it did and why it chose to do that in the first place.

What is upstairs' view about the death penalty?

Upstairs' view about man choosing to kill his fellow man for any reason whatsoever, is that such an action is… inappropriate. We don't do judgements, so it's not for me to say it's wrong or bad. It is inappropriate. It's not the way the system was intended. Mankind was designed to live cooperatively, collaboratively, helpfully, love thy neighbour. That's the utopian lifestyle and community culture that we had hoped to achieve.

When I say man taking the life of another man, I include war in that. I include murder, manslaughter; I include the death penalty. I exclude euthanasia.

You have to then say – what about accidental killings?

Let's say somebody's out game hunting but a human gets hit. The difference here comes back to intent. A true accident of that nature was never intended. It was something that went dreadfully wrong. Even though a life has been lost and a soul has been catapulted unexpectedly back up here, there was never any intent on the part of the person who pulled that trigger. You could say the same about a car accident. If two cars hit each other and one driver dies, there was never any intent on the part of the first driver to kill the other.

With the death penalty, the State intends and proactively chooses to end a life. In the way humans were, we now say idealistically, designed that was never ever part of the plan.

Going back to the game hunting for a moment, animals are there to be the food chain. Animals understand that. Humans used to know and understand that. Some ethnic cultures still understand and appreciate that. But killing animals for sport is not part of what was ever designed. Why for heaven's sake? If you were killing them to eat and feed families, then that's part of the grand design. It's about intent and it was never ever designed that way either. We don't like it – no that's being judgemental. We don't approve but it's not for us to judge. It's for humans to run their own world.

What about the souls of people who have been responsible for genocides? Modern names include Hitler, Stalin, Mao Zedong, Pol Pot. Why would they come in with that intent and are they treated any differently when they return?

Gosh, this is really heavy stuff. Let me answer the easier bit first. Once they come back up here they go through exactly the same process as everyone else. They have a rest and recovery period, they do their review but these will be skewed, as all reviews are, towards assessing whether this life met the goals set out in the soul plan. That question has to be addressed even when people like these folk have done the horrendous things that they've done. I cannot even get my head around why someone would have genocide on their soul plan. I cannot, in any shape or form, in all my thousands of years up here, I cannot conceive why…

Let's step back from the emotion. Firstly, you have to say, was it in the soul plan?

Maybe they went in with a need to do control in a big way. Now there are many ways that humans can manifest control. You can be a chief executive of a company; you can be a heavy-handed policeman; you can be a tyrant in your own home. Instigating genocide has got to be the most extreme manifestation of controlling as many people as you possibly can to the ultimate extreme of killing them all. It must come from massive control issues.

Let's assume that genocide is not on their soul plan but control to a major degree is – although why that would be there I can't quite conceive either. It might be to balance very submissive past lives; I could see that as being plausible. Let's say they had been a slave and had to put up with brutality as a slave in more than one life. Now they come back to experience the opposite which is being in control.

Then you have to ask – once they're in human form, has this control gone to their heads; has the ego gone overboard? Did some of these people have some physiological or mental condition, were they manic or did they have a psychiatric condition? That has to be possible as well.

I can understand control being in a plan. Control is an equally valid human experience and genocide is the worst extreme of that, but the perpetrators lose sight of what they're doing. They've long since lost sight of the fact that they're killing fellow human beings.

Hitler's aim was to have a pure white state and, in his view, the Jewish folk did not meet his criteria. It's wartime and the whole of Europe is topsy-turvy… I can't speak for Hitler or any of them; I can only guess. So under the cover of war where horrendous things are happening anyway, he quietly ships them off and gets rid of them permanently.

I have to assume that all of these people genuinely believed that they did what they did for the right reasons. Hitler truly believed in his white Aryan state and that this was the way Germany should be. Although upstairs we view his actions as totally abhorrent, he must have believed that he was doing the right things for the right reasons for the right end-goal. Now that has to say that his thinking has become extremely skewed. One example is enough – it's all too ghastly to even think about.

It surprises me that this bestiality is allowed.

How do you stop someone like that? I suppose we talk about Hitler because his actions are well documented and moderately well known. There are plenty of others who are less well known.

With Pol Pot, it was thousands of skeletons.

They all had thousands of skeletons on their hands – and not just those four we just mentioned. There have been plenty of others in the 20th century as well. What about the Rwandan genocide? But you can also go back – what about the Crusaders? They weren't exactly angels – on either side of that era.

Did the victims of any genocide have a prior agreement to all die together collectively under these same circumstances? Could you call them a karmic group?

Oh, my god… that is huge – but good. I think the answer is yes and no. Because we talked mostly about Hitler I will continue with him merely to illustrate. The principles are pretty much the same for any group of genocide victims.

With all those unfortunate Jewish folk who died in the gas chambers or prisoner-of-war camps, there will have been karmic groups within that mass of people. They might have been families, often extended families. It's really hard in human understanding terms to say that they had agreed to this before they incarnated but they had. All the victims had agreed to die in those horrendous fashions.

Now that is just inconceivable really. To even try to get some understanding, let alone acceptance of that statement, you have to try and see the bigger picture, even beyond Hitler. What followed after the Second World War was that Hitler was defeated and the fact that all those people died became public knowledge wider across Europe towards the end of the war.

After the war, the surviving Jewish folk became extremely adamant about demanding their own home territory. Out of those demands came the state of Israel. For thousands of years, there has been conflict over the occupation of that site because the three Abrahamic religions [Judaism, Islam and Christianity] all have some rightful claim (bad word) to the significance of Jerusalem in particular, in their history and their culture. If you go back, had the gas chambers not existed and six million Jewish people not died, there would not have been that Jewish backlash after the war and Israel would not necessarily have come into being in the way it did.

All those folk who died had some understanding that by agreeing to death by this means, they were hopeful that some sort of resolution to Jewish homelands would come about as a consequence. They could only be hopeful because human free-will always dictates the actions and outcomes and they have no control over what happens after they've died anyway.

Now in human terms – how on earth can you conceive that six million souls would all agree up here, some separately, some as groups, to undergo this horrendous ending?

Of course, once you're in human form you forget this deeper purpose and they were subjected to the most appalling, inhuman, brutal, barbaric ending, as is now public knowledge.

Then you might ask – how could we orchestrate to get so many souls all to agree to this, more or less at the same time?

Many of them were youngsters who died, others were in their sixties and older, and every age in between. Because there was at least a sixty-year age range, we could stagger the soul planning over that same time span.

Well, we achieved the front end of that objective. The gas chambers, horrendous as they were, achieved the creation of the Jewish state of Israel. That was the purpose behind that particular genocide. Huge, and really hard to understand.

Now you have to say – what about the other genocides that have come about in the world? Pol Pot?

That genocide ended up with his undoing and in time the country returned to its own culture. At a human level, any genocide is the most horrendous vehicle for achieving major cultural and civil change. Huge, in human sacrifice terms.

Chapter 5
THE DISCARNATE SOUL

Can you paint some sort of picture about the environment upstairs, please?

There is no physical picture to paint because there is no physical. There are all manner of different beings throughout the whole universe. They all exist in different fashions. They take on different roles and do different things. From the perspective of a human image, it's just like a big empty nothingness. There is nothing because it is all ethereal, all just energy.

If it is just ethereal energy, how do I know where a particular soul is and who he is and how he is and where to find him? It's an issue about recognition of souls which is not physical. We don't have eyes and peer across the room.

To be honest, to try and paint a picture would be beyond human understanding. The mechanism clearly exists. I know spontaneously where someone is. I can just go *ping*, like that and be with him. There is no way of expressing in human language how I recognise him, how I know where he is and how I get there instantly. How do I know it's

David and not Frank or Margaret or someone else? I just can't do that in terms that humans would understand.

Let me try to give you an analogy. In your human terms, if you were to ask a tribesman who had only lived in the Amazonian jungle completely isolated from the rest of the world, what the whole planet was like, he could only tell you about his own environment. He may well assume that the whole planet is just his local area. He has no means of knowing, let alone understanding that there is anything more never mind what happens anywhere else. If you did explain the rest of the world to him he couldn't even understand the very words you were using and he would just look totally blank with incomprehension.

What happens when a soul returns?

Although I have already touched on this, let me elaborate. Each soul is given the appropriate amount of rest and support it needs first. The traumatised soul is almost the extreme of how much rest is needed. An ordinary soul/human who sat on his couch, went to work and raised the kids will go almost immediately straight through to a review because there has been nothing radical or drastic in its life.

By the time any soul does its review, it is hopefully in a place of calm energy where it's distant enough from the emotion but can remember the events and the reactions enough to rationally evaluate them. That's what we're trying to do. That's why traumatised souls are given this rest period to start with. From that evaluation, the soul can learn and think about what it wants to do next.

If you're going to review anything, up here or down on earth, you have to remember the circumstances and the situation. If your politicians are going to assess some major event by doing a Senate Inquiry or Royal Commission then everybody has to remember, and contribute what they remember, to make some analysis of that situation. It's the same up here.

We have to take those remembrances back in order to conduct that review.

The review is held with a group of people, let's call them a panel and, unlike your panels or juries in a court, these are absolutely non-judgemental. Up here nobody has the position or seniority or authority to judge. You sit with your panel and they will ask, what do you think about that? What do you think about this?

When you return, you also bring back your soul plan which, although you have forgotten it during the human incarnation, is still deep in your consciousness because that is what has guided your human actions and circumstances. If your soul plan included getting knocked down by a bus, for instance, the soul sets you up for that. When the time comes, the soul recalls that from the plan in order to get the physical you into a position to be hit by the bus. Then the human free-will in you will say, do I want to be knocked down by this bus or not? You either lie down in front of the bus or jump to one side. That's an extreme example.

When you do the review, you remember the soul plan as the goal posts that you set and wanted to reach. All the activity that happened during that life was aimed at reaching those goal posts. The panel will help you by saying that if the goal was to get run over by a bus but you didn't achieve it, why was that? Then you have to think about why and discuss it as a group. You either come to your own conclusions or whatever the answers are, or you are gently guided to go and think about it.

That then leads on to what happens next. If you have majorly not met any or many of your goals, you will very likely be encouraged to think about a new incarnation relatively soon to have another go at meeting them.

Does that complement of energies or qualities within a soul change as a result of a human life and lives?

The answer can be yes and no. Yes, if you have achieved the goals.

If you set out to be run over by this blessed bus – you would only set a goal that radical for very good reasons. What would you learn from being run over by a bus? Perhaps I picked a bad example here. To trust that it was meant to be perhaps? The traumatic ending? That's a good one. Let's just stick with those two.

To trust that it was meant to be even though in human terms that's hugely hard to accept. Let's say you needed to experience a traumatic, fast, sharp ending. You allowed yourself up to be hit by the bus which meant that you died and passed very quickly. Therefore, when you're doing the review, it's clear that you have met that particular goal post. From that experience, you take away the higher learning from that situation, so you can now assess and absorb that knowledge.

Let's say the learning was about trusting that it was meant to be. Because you trusted, you allowed the bus to hit you and you died, you can now see the learning about trust or trusting. That trusting component within your soul bubble is now enhanced both in strength and possibly in percentage terms. If the trusting energy was five per cent of your soul before you incarnated, it might now be six per cent, just to illustrate. But it also might be a stronger five or six per cent. It's two-dimensional in its change.

Then you say – if my soul's energy bubble was one hundred per cent in total when I incarnated into that life, now that I've come back with this enlarged component, does that mean something else has diminished?

You don't go down with just one objective. Or you might go down with a fairly singular but huge goal. In a case like that, you will have sub-goals underneath like a pyramid. Your plan might be to meet all of the lower ones so they can come together into the big one.

Virtually no soul ever achieves all of its objectives or sub-goals. Let's stick with the same soul who's been run over by the bus, but let's say he also set himself a goal about honesty. He needed to be so super-honest that he wouldn't even take a pencil from the office.

He ends up being, we won't make him a burglar but let's say he takes lots of stationary from the office or occasionally would walk out of a restaurant without paying or didn't pay his fare on the train; all minor things but they're still issues about honesty. When he goes back after this bus accident, on one hand, he's got a plus in the trusting component, but over here he's got a minus in honesty.

Overall it jiggles around and balances. We don't have anything quite as finite as your concept of a hundred per cent. We're not that rigid. If it was a hundred and one per cent or more or less, that's all about energy being fluid.

When you're planning to come down again, do you bring the goals that you didn't reach before?

You might and let's continue with that honesty theme. He might decide for himself (because nobody tells him) that he really mucked up on this honesty goal and it might be sufficiently significant… maybe he's had past lives where he was a burglar or a murderer or something dreadful. This time he needs to balance that but he's failed a little bit because he's still taking things like free train rides. Because of his history, he might say that's still a big enough concern that he would come back and have another go at trying to do honesty. He wouldn't need to come back to do trusting again because he's achieved that one. It's almost like your to-do list where you can cross this off but down here there are all these other things you can't tick off yet.

Now, in addition to that, a human who is learning in this way (not a couch potato who is not learning) will have experiences up here and find new things he wants to learn. As you will read, Ben with his technology is a fabulous example. In all his time up here, Ben's been able to watch and latterly talk to you about computer technology which could never have been part of his original soul complement. Because he has a strong analytical quality he can see how the technology could be used in a really major fashion.

You might say that a new energy component has been added to his soul which is to do with the technology. The driver for this life is to satisfy this new soul component. As you will read, he's also taking forward the qualities of cross-cultural tolerance. Karmically he doesn't need to repeat a life in order to get better at that but he carries it forward as a benefit and a positive contribution. Then with this new unsatisfied energy, he's going to use those old strengths to help satisfy this new need.

The composition of a soul's energy can change in all of those ways. New ones can be added, existing ones can be satisfied – they don't go away, they're satisfied. Those that have failed to be fulfilled because the goals haven't been met in a life, remain unsatisfied and have to be done again until those goals are met and that energy is satisfied.

Do souls ever fulfil all of their goals? If that happens, what happens to the soul after that or do they find new goals?

Increasingly in the last two hundred years, slowly starting from the Industrial Revolution, souls have sat up here and watched the developments on earth and got hooked on the idea that they could help or contribute. They would find new goals based around say, steam engines or whatever it might be, the engineering that went into the *Titanic* for instance. Increasing numbers of souls are finding new goals, driven or prompted by these developments. Some who might have satisfied all they had to do, are putting their hand up and saying, "I want to have a go at something else."

I suspect that might also have been the case in times of prior civilisations, let's say like Atlantis where there were certainly all the technological developments for crystalline power sources. That evolved; it didn't just suddenly pop into somebody's head one day. I guess that souls sitting up here then would have seen that and said, "I want to have a go at that too." Souls can sit back for a long time and then suddenly say, "I want to have a go at this."

Now that doesn't answer the whole question. The first question – is there a finite limit to the number of goals and learnings that a soul must do, or does it go on infinitely?

Virtually every soul will have a very large number of goals over thousands upon thousands of years. As I said before, virtually no soul ever achieves all its goals in any one lifetime. It comes back with leftovers, sometimes it comes back with some it could have done better at and others that it can cross off its list, or a mixture of all that. You can spend aeons reincarnating before you ever get anywhere near ticking them all off. Then you can suddenly discover a new one and the list suddenly gets extended again.

That, therefore, says that the reincarnation cycle continues forever and doesn't ever stop.

What happens when a gay soul returns?

Every single soul goes through the same process once it returns. The only thing that varies between any two extremes, let's say, Mother Theresa who's done all this good, good, good, and Jack the Ripper who's done all this bad, bad, bad, is the content of that review. A Mother-Theresa-type person will assess why she's gone overboard doing so much good; the murderer Jack the Ripper will evaluate why he's gone to the totally opposite extreme of doing so much dreadfully bad stuff.

The review of a soul who has lived a gay life will only be skewed toward looking at whether that life met the needs of its soul plan. That's what every review is about. You had the plan to play this game. The goal post was over there. The plan was to kick ten goals, did you meet the ten goals? Pretty simple. Although the goals will vary enormously, that's all the review is doing. Irrespective of whether you're gay or a murderer or an Eskimo, the process is the same.

When a traumatised soul is doing its review, is that trauma going to be the strongest component in the bubble?

Not necessarily. Going back to my soldier killed in war, the first thing that happens is that it will get maximum support and go for a long period of rest to recuperate which is almost the equivalent of the grieving you do while you are still in human form. It will be comforted and supported until its bubble energy graph, including the trauma, has come back to a level field. Then it's ready to do the review – there's no point asking it to do that while it's so traumatised. You can't be logical or rational when you're in that state.

Is it fair to say that the majority of souls are ordinary folk who only need to live for work, marriage and raising the kids?

Yes, that's absolutely right. For every major significant person in any country or any field, and not just politics, for every Gandhi, there must have been hundreds of thousands of ordinary folk in his country. For every Beethoven, there must be hundreds of thousands of pianists and composers. Different examples in any field. For every Einstein, there are trillions of scientists all over the world who would love to be as bright as he was. But by definition, the vast majority are (I hate the phrase) ordinary folk.

For work, marriage and raising children?

Yes. I'm quite happy to confirm that this is not to diminish that role. There is still plenty for those folk to learn from having many lives as a family member or a single person with children and living fairly normal lives doing ordinary things. It's not a role that is diminished in any sense.

What do ordinary souls, the majority of humanity, do between incarnations?

I think this links in with a question about – what do people do in a long gap between lives? This gets difficult. It also implies – do ordinary folk do different things when they're up here, from significant people who've been Einstein or Mozart for instance.

Some people will choose, be guided, to reincarnate fairly quickly and that could be for reasons such as a long list of things they didn't achieve this time or previously. They may have brought back energies of new things they want to try next time. Maybe in that life, they were touched by, or on the edge of, or seen the wonders of modern technology and they want to have a go with that.

Conversely, they could say, "I need to consolidate everything I've learnt and I do not want or need and I can't cope with a new incarnation soon." (Consolidation is a good word). So they will go off, be quiet and reflect and just do gentle things until they've worked that through. At the end of that, they might come back and have another think about what they want to do next or whether some special role up here might help their learning. They might then want to reincarnate soon-ish.

What have significant people all done in their two-thousand-year gap and why so long?

Now it can sound like a cop out when I say that two thousand years is but a blink up here because that doesn't answer the question. We all know how much has happened on your planet earth in two thousand years — a mighty lot.

On the whole, people who have waited a long period will be old souls with wisdom who don't have a great need to come back in a hurry. They can afford to wait — if they ever come back — because they only have a much shorter list of things still to tick off so it doesn't matter if they wait two thousand years or more.

Folk who have been significant in a life will have the choice of having some sort of guiding and helping role up here. They've been significant in those lives because they are already learned souls with wisdom.

Now a Beethoven or a Mozart is very learned and has much wisdom about the writing and playing of music. Even though they incarnated as ordinary souls like everyone else, a huge element in their soul bubble is music, its creativity and appreciation. After their return they might then have a guiding role amongst souls which have a need to learn about music — souls can learn up here before and after an incarnation. Old souls are doing things up here as well as not having a great need to rush back.

Let's say an ordinary soul incarnates and his mother makes him learn the piano. He likes it and goes on to do music at university. He's not a Mozart but he's still quite good. When he comes back he reviews that life and decides that he wants to keep doing more music. There will be somebody like the names you know, to help and guide him with that. Folk like Einstein with his strong analytical and scientific brain will be helping souls who want to be scientists or mathematicians or both. People like Gandhi, like Jesus, like Muhammad, will have a guiding role in spiritual or religious fields.

Digressing for a moment – what religious leaders had in common was that they were trying to espouse good and the right ways of doing things for the community in which they lived. Even Moses with his long list of 'thou shalt and thou shalt not', was trying to do the right thing for his peoples. They all evolved different versions of what that might be but they were all wanting to make life easier and better for ordinary people and they found these spiritual ways of trying to help.

Sticking with Christianity for the moment, it wasn't Jesus who started it at all. It was everyone afterwards. Jesus' philosophy was love-thy-neighbour and deep down, Islam is also a peace-based religion. They're all about peace and harmony and well-being in a community. Leaving aside where Islam has gone from Muhammad's day and where it has gone since Jesus' day, they all have this quality of wanting, through gentle community caring, peace-based means, to bring welfare and harmony to their peoples.

Coming back to the question – younger souls up here who have a strong inclination in those directions will go and get guidance from any of these experienced souls.

We do have different roles up here. Because there are so many on earth, more and more are dying rapidly so there is a greater need for support roles when they first come back. There are more and more of us working in that capacity too, helping to ease that transition, getting them oriented back into existence up here. All sorts of different things go on up here.

Once a soul has lived one (or more than one) significant life, does it continue to choose lives that will be significant or can future lives be ordinary?

Most souls which have been significant, need to have lots of ordinary lives as a balance. Socrates or Pythagoras for example, who did all those intellectual things – they were great intellects, particularly for their time –

they will have wanted to do a lot of ordinary lives, particularly as women, as family men and wives, in different circumstances, in poverty, wealth, different places, to balance those enormous lives. Because these two both had big intellects they might come back later on as another great intellectual. In theory – in reality, I have no idea – one of them might have come back as somebody like Einstein who must have had the most amazing brain as well. They might have come back as a woman with a big brain, somebody like Marie Curie. (I use these names just as examples to illustrate.)

Why do some souls choose to return almost instantly?

Most often this is because the soul has chosen to have another go at achieving goals which it previously had failed at or hadn't done as well as it needed to.

But sometimes there can be a theme that carries forward from one life to the next and it may be that the soul wants to experience both sides of that theme in quick succession. Let me explain using Anthea's three most recent lives which were all back-to-back effectively. This is a theme about atomic energy and its use.

> In the 1940s Anthea lived a life as a male atomic energy researcher. He worked in Los Alamos [the US site that developed the bombs that were dropped on Japan at the end of the Second World War]. In that life, he (and others) spoke out strongly against developing these bombs but they were ignored. He died at a young age as a consequence of exposure to radiation.
>
> Almost immediately she reincarnated as a child living in Hiroshima where, at the age of four, she died instantly the day that the bomb was dropped. So violent was this death that the body was physically

vaporised, nothing left at all, and her soul along with thousands of others, instantly hurtled through the ether up here. That was in August 1945.

Less than two years later she was born into this life where her only passion at school was atomic physics and her first career was as a medical radiographer. So what is the connection? Well, medical radiography uses x-rays (another form of atomic energy) for humanitarian purposes, for making helpful, medical decisions which will enhance and prolong life, not maim and kill.

You can see how in these three lives she was able to experience the various sides to that theme, the death and destruction versus the positive and life-enhancing.

These three lives were planned together. By that I mean they were part of one long over-arching plan that was designed to play out over these three incarnations.

What is a ghost?

In your human world, there are places like mountains and lakes that have a naturally-occurring, special energy. There are also places that are cold, dark, damp and spooky, and have negative, cringey feelings to them. This eerie, scary energy is mostly felt in man-made places, not often in nature. You would say that kind of feeling has a weird, unnerving feel to it; the sort place that you would call haunted. So, what is haunted and what is going on here?

Often places like that are dilapidated, run-down, empty, devoid of any human – and often animal too – activity in many a long year. The soul of that place is dying, shrinking. It's disintegrating physically and therefore the energy that was in the timber, in the building, in the ground underneath or in the roof above is lost. It is just shrivelling which is why you get this horrible sensation to it. You don't necessarily get that feeling because there is a stuck soul.

Now the question is – is a ghost a soul that is stuck in the first place?

Sometimes the answer is yes and sometimes no. Sometimes souls don't want to leave. Sometimes they are so attached to the human who they've spent the last umpteen years with that they really, really don't want to go. A few of them will be attached to the extent that they will try and find a mechanism for staying around the place where that human was. They will inhabit that building or house or church or whatever it happens to be. If the human has been buried (not cremated) in a cemetery or churchyard, they will sometimes hang around that area because that's where their human is now and they really want to maintain that contact. If the cemetery is near the house, they might flit between the two.

They chose to stay. They're not stuck in the physical sense that somebody has to release them. The idea of doing an exorcism to release a soul that is trapped, is a bit erroneous. The soul will remain of its own choice. Every soul knows that it has to go back at some stage but these few are so reluctant to leave – they're not reluctant to return, they're just reluctant to leave – for reasons to do with attachment to their human. That can go on for hundreds of years but eventually, the call to return becomes sufficiently strong that they acknowledge that it's time to leave. Quite what it achieves by hanging around for hundreds of years, I am at a loss to understand.

If you have a soul inhabiting a building that is collapsing, unlived in and its energy is dissipating, you've got this double dose of energies. Dissipating physical energy and the energy of this soul which remains (I'm not going to use the word stuck) is a bit distorted as well. Deep down it knows it should have gone back but it's just hanging on and hanging on. So its energy has got a bit cock-eyed too and that can permeate.

So these unusual, not negative but just not pleasant, energies hang around these particular spaces. If a human is sensitive to energies, they will sense that there is something odd going on. The idea of seeing ghosts as humans who walk through walls and all that sort of stuff is a bit fanciful.

When you've been in that situation, there's nothing fanciful about it.

Of course, the human genuinely believes that's what they have seen. But from the soul's point of view, they don't need to take on the image of a human to be there. They are just there. It's just a combination of these unpleasant, unnatural, energies in unusual places that generate this sense of what you call haunted.

What are spirit guides? How do they get assigned to a person? How many typically? Can they be souls you have shared a past life with?

Spirit guides are souls up here who have agreed to support and guide and be a prop, a back-stop for you if that's what's needed. When you're planning your next incarnation finding those guides is part of the process. Typically you would ask souls who you had shared past lives with and with whom you had had good experiences, souls who were (your concept of) really good mates. In another time and place, you would then be very happy to be a spirit guide for them in return.

Spirit guides may also be angels, archangels, ascended masters or other senior beings whose role through all eternity is to be a spirit guide. They would be in addition to the souls that you have chosen. To illustrate:

I, Saint-Germaine, am one of Anthea's spirit guides and that is because, aeons back, we shared a life or lives and, in this incarnation, I have agreed to do this. She also has other spirit guides who are folk she has shared other lives with. They have agreed to remain discarnate and be her backup support, mentor, guide while she is incarnate.

How many does anyone have?

It varies enormously. It's never likely to be just one because there is no backstop if something happens to that one. So it likely to be a minimum of several through to maybe ten or a dozen or even fifteen; I've not really thought about it before. If a soul has come to do a gentle life experiencing ordinary things, it might have a handful, three, four, five, but if it's come to do important work, it will have heaps.

Are guardian angels the same thing?

My sense is that it's a terminology issue. The concept that humans tend to understand as guardian angels, is pretty much the same as I described for spirit guides.

Chapter 6

WALK-INS

What is a walk-in?

Although I have now described the whole soul cycle, I still need to explain walk-ins, which is a new-ish, special concept and is directly relevant to Ben's story. He incarnated by way of a walk-in.

Every living human body has a soul from around the time of birth in the same way that it has two arms and ten toes, but a few adults have an additional soul.

A walk-in is an incarnation just like any other except that the returning soul decides that it wants to come back into a human at the age of twelve or twenty (or whatever) rather than at the age of zero. Now you could say therefore, this physical person has got two souls, his original and the walk-in. With Tobias[4], Sam had his own soul for the first

---

[4] Tobias was a soul who channelled through Geoffrey Hoppe from Crimson Circle for ten years until it incarnated via a walk-in to an American lad called Sam in 2009.

twelve years of his life and then Tobias joined in. So does Sam have two souls floating around in his body? Is that a conflict or a problem?

It's a bit more fluid than that because a soul is only energy and even though it is discreet in some ways, it's very easy for energy to blend. When the sun heats a stone and the stone gets warm for example, that's energy that has blended.

What happens is that while the two souls are incarnate in that body, they will usually blend together for the best outcome for the physical person but also to meet their own needs. When a walk-in happens, the souls' boundaries will blur and the energies will meld together like that (fingers intertwine to illustrate). They've already agreed to what degree because they've both decided what they need to learn and experience from this particular walk-in. They will then go through that life as a blended soul.

How and why did the idea of a walk-in evolve?

Somewhere in his story Ben rightly observes, "Your world is in such a mess that it needs people, souls, sooner rather than later." Up here folk started to realise this and that, therefore, we needed to be able to get more souls down on earth quickly. So we had to devise more complex, flexible and fluid arrangements.

The question then became – how are we going to do this without ending up with an over-population which brings different problems and does not solve our need to get more souls down there.

There was a committee which discussed it at great length and many ideas were put on the table. A walk-in was the end result and it has been a very satisfactory solution.

As part of that process, the committee said that for this to work, the discarnate soul has to be able to communicate with the already-incarnate soul at the planning stage. Firstly, the host soul (that's a lovely phrase) needs to agree to have an incomer coming in. It's already there. It has first choice. It has to agree to share the space. If it doesn't want to do that, it has to have the prerogative to say sorry mate. That was one of the first rules that we set up. In order for the two souls to have that discussion, there has to be some sort of communication mechanism.

How can that happen when once any soul has incarnated, there is no celestial intervention?

The answer is complicated. Yes, that's true with the single exception that any walk-in is able to have that communication while it is still discarnate. Let me back-track.

It's like a fine tube… (bad word but it's the only way I can describe it). There's this narrow mechanism which allows the discarnate soul to access the incarnate host soul – a speaking tube is a human equivalent. Both souls have one end of it and it's structured so they can communicate wholly and only for the purpose of discussing whether this walk-in is agreeable to both of them and then to work out how and when. They need to plan it between them. If the discarnate soul suddenly asked what the football scores were, there would be nothing coming back.

It's a very narrow field of discussion; it's very controlled and very limited. That communication channel does not close off until the walk-in soul has incarnated. Once it has moved in with the host soul, there is no need for the channel and it closes off in both of them. After that, neither soul will have any celestial intervention.

That then begs the question – did Tom's[5] host soul know before he incarnated that there was a chance of a walk-in?

---

[5] Tom is the physical human into whom Ben walked in.

In that particular case, the answer is yes. Both of them. When Ben and the host soul were still discarnate, they could communicate in the normal fashion up here. The host soul must have put his hand up and said he was willing to discuss it. He was willing to be on the list – and that's effectively what it is – to share a physical body with a walk-in if that proved to be appropriate and necessary. Because he was willing, that communication mechanism was established before he left and at the time he incarnated it became open and available.

Now I have no idea whether that is then open and available to souls other than Ben, who might also choose to be a walk-in to Tom instead. I have to assume that multiple discarnate souls are able to discuss the possibility of being his walk-in.

Let's say Helen over here decides that this same host soul would be appropriate for her needs and this time she wants to come back as a walk-in. She too might talk to our host soul and between them, they might decide no, it's not a good match. Whereas Ben talks in the same way and the two of them decide, yes this is a good match. After that agreement is made, other souls can't talk. It's closed off to them. That's one host soul that's crossed off the list and is no longer available. The two souls then get on with the business of planning and managing the why's and wherefores leading up to the point of the walk-in.

Therefore, both Ben and the host soul knew that at, probably at age fourteen, fifteen or sixteen, they could expect to come together?

Yes, that would have all been part of them conversing about where and when and those discussions would have gone on over a very long period. When the walk-in is still discarnate, the discussion is all about the planning and the timing for that to happen. Everything that needs to be worked out once both souls are in the physical happens after the walk-in has incarnated.

From here on the question is – how does that communication happen now and if you really want to get complicated – how does it happen once they are melded?

They think together and they work it out together and communicate telepathically. There will be circumstances where one wants to do something because it meets his soul needs but the other one won't be so strong on it. They still have to work it out but it will be in a more fluid sense.

Are walk-ins confined to certain ages?

Yes, they are really. They have to happen by early adulthood at the latest. By this age, the host soul has learnt all the childhood and early teens stuff that the walk-in wishes to avoid. By coming in at early adulthood, they start out on the human's adult path together. If the walk-in came in at the age of thirty let's say, the host soul has already had ten or fifteen years of living and experiencing adulthood, is set in its way and understands how the human needs to operate. It would be a big ask to expect the host soul Firstly, to accommodate the walk-in and then try to teach or guide or help it with all the adult stuff. By coming together in early adulthood, they mutually learn the adult paths and experiences.

Also, by joining at thirty, a walk-in is potentially missing a lot. If the human had a car accident and died at the age of twenty-five, well, it's missed the boat altogether.

The timing is for both of those reasons and to maximise the opportunities. It's based on what it wants to experience and the timing is in line with the needs in its soul plan.

Have walk-ins ever shared past lives with their host souls?

I think the answer is yes and no because the question that leads on from that it is – how do walk-ins choose their soul partners?

Ben talks about how he chose his soul-partner. My understanding is that they had not shared a past life but chose each other because they shared the same sort of soul goals for this incarnation. That has to be the obvious reason for choosing any host soul. There is always this common feature of having a shared goal or goals.

In that sense, if the two souls in a walk-in had previously shared a life, not necessarily as a walk-in, and had worked together but had failed to reach their goal, they might decide to come back as a walk-in feeling that their melded souls might be a stronger force for achieving that goal.

This is a logical extension of karmic groups and we talked about whether karmic groups had previously shared past lives. If members of a karmic group, maybe some but not all, have failed to achieve a common goal, or not achieved it as well as they would have liked, they might choose to come back and have another go at that same goal. Under those conditions, they might choose to come back as a walk-in feeling that a melded soul will have a stronger influence and therefore everyone has a better chance of achieving that goal. That's the most logical reason.

It's like a stepping process. The first step is that we share past lives in which we may or may not work together. The second step is that we come back as a karmic group, small in number, where we aim to achieve a common goal but we don't do as well as we'd hoped. The third step is that two of us come back as a walk-in to have another go at achieving that same goal.

When a melded walk-in soul flies off at night, does it unmeld and each soul go its own way or do they stay melded?

They stay together. If a situation arises where one soul wants to go and talk to his friends and the other also wants to do that too, then they work out an agreement between them. One night they will talk to one set of friends, and another night they will talk to the other's friends.

If tonight they go and see the walk-in's friends, then the host soul will be an integral part of that. The friends will know that he is a walk-in and they will welcome the host soul to join the conversation if he wishes. Sometimes the host soul will feel that he has nothing to contribute because they're talking about old times or unknown mutual friends. If you go to a party where you know nobody, it's very hard to join in when they're all talking about mutual friends. Other times you might go to a party where you know quite a lot of people so it's easy to talk to them because you have a shared background and other friends in common.

After they have been melded for long enough there will be enough common ground that there will be things that they both want to do and share as well.

When the physical body dies, do both souls go back?

One or other might have chosen to leave before the end. Let's go back to Tobias. Tobias went in when Sam was twelve and he's now around twenty. Theoretically, Tobias may have only wanted to experience teenage-hood and the twenties. He might have decided that when Sam gets to be around thirty, let's say, he's done everything he needs to do and he might leave.

Would Sam know that he's left?

No. In the same way that Sam was not particularly aware that he had come. If you remember, Sam fell off his bike and was in the hospital. He was physically and mentally low and in a bit of shock which made it easy for Tobias to blend in. You could conceive that something similar happens in reverse. Maybe Sam just gets ill, something that just takes him out of the mainstream of his life and lays him low for a bit – it doesn't have to be as drastic as an accident – and Tobias can gently drift off.

Can a human have three or more souls that have all walked in?

No, for the simple reason that a physical body has only got so much finite space within and between its cells. An adult human obviously has a lot more cells, and therefore a lot more space, than a new-born infant.

As a child grows there are more cells because the cells multiply. Let's say that a child has a soul in which intellect is ten per cent, just to illustrate. When the child is newborn, let's say that only a tenth of that full-sized intellect component will come in because that's all the available physical space and all the need there is. As the child physically grows, more space develops and more soul will just slowly move and blend in. By the time it's physically adult size and shape, the whole soul will have flowed in bit by bit. But what flows each time is a little bit more of everything, not just one component followed by another.

There's no room for more than two and it's also in part for those physical, practical reasons that they will meld. The melded pair will take less space than the two separately.

Anthea has been the subject of a walk-in in this life so let's look at that to illustrate.

> Mark was a friend of Anthea's in this life and they had shared several past lives, one where he was her son and another where he was her superior. They had a prior soul agreement that he would be a walk-in for

her after his death. They planned and agreed to this before either of them incarnated.

Mark had a long, protracted illness which left him increasingly physically debilitated before he finally died in 2009. During that period his soul spent a good nine months flitting back and forth to visit her, to try before you buy, putting his toe in the water. Even though he, or they, had agreed to this walk-in at a soul level, he was still thinking "...er, do I really want to do this?" Then he'd go away and think about it some more. "Well, I did make a commitment," so he'd come back and try again. For him, a lot of it was around the idea of being in a female body, so quickly after sixty-odd years as a male. He was very strong-willed, a strong character.

After he physically died, he still took a long time to fully integrate into Anthea. Part of this was getting used to being in a female body but it was also his need to spend time upstairs doing his review of the life he'd just left. He needed to fit in both, balance both before he got totally absorbed into Anthea's life.

What they've done now is that they've blended. His intellect and other characteristics have integrated with hers but that was largely the purpose. He was extremely intelligent and very self-confident so he's bought some of those qualities to her as well. There's been a definite blurring and blending.

So you see, there are degrees. Tobias went in wholly, lock stock and barrel to Sam. Mark took a long time to integrate what he needed to and he's pretty much all in with her now.

Normally a walk-in is much quicker not taking six or nine months and certainly not with a prolonged try-before-you-buy. It would have been a good eighteen months from his early visits to full integration which is really unusual in my observation. It would be more like Tobias. *Bing.* In. We're there. Then we just get on with what we've come to do.

Now all this is contrary to what I just said about a walk-in only joining in early adulthood. The first thing to say is that this particular arrangement is an exception rather than the rule. The Mark walk-in was designed to complement and enhance Anthea's strengths and skills at this particular age and stage when the plan was that she would be doing this work.

The purpose and point for him behind this particular incarnation was to add his strength and intelligence to her, to give her more stamina and ability to cope with the physical aspects of this work at this later point in her life. By that, I mean more particularly the marketing, website, publishing, the editing, all the stuff that follows. If she is doing this in her mid- or late-70s, she will need as much extra stamina and mental and physical and emotional support as she can get.

[At the time this was going on, I was physically unaware of Mark. It was through a hot Australian summer and I was packing up my house before moving, so my whole attention and energies were focused on meeting the moving deadline and surviving the heat.]

Mark

Well, this channelling is a new experience which I haven't done independently since she and I became one.

I have been totally involved in this journey of creating this book and having Saint-Germaine tell us all these wonderful answers. I have to say I never expected to get into these realms when I agreed to be her walk-in. I have enjoyed it enormously and it has challenged my intellect. I am grateful to her for that aspect because it is a totally unexpected pleasure and bonus. In that sense, it has been a very pleasurable and interesting journey so far and my sense is that it will go on for quite some many years yet.

Maybe you would like to hear what it's been like for me as a walk-in since this book is also about walk-ins.

> In the many months leading up to my moving in permanently, I did come and dip my toe in the water. I had some quite strong reservations about doing this in part because she is female and I had just been a strong-willed and very independent male. I lived that life on my terms. I hope I wasn't so bad that I put that before other people's needs but I was fairly self-focused. In my work life, I had lots of freedom which I enjoyed and in later years enough money which allowed me to travel and do lots of things independently. In the end, I had financial independence and intellectual independence. I did not have a boss telling that I had to think or work in a certain way. My intellect, therefore, had free reign to think about what new things would be beneficial to my work situation.
>
> When I got ill and was told that this illness would be a long slow physical deterioration, it took me quite some time to get over the shock of that. I'm not sure that my wife ever really got over it, to be honest. She was the most amazingly wonderful carer. I was ill for about nine months, perhaps up to a year. I couldn't have asked for more help or support or love or dedication. Absolutely phenomenal. I feel unbelievably blessed and still emotional all this time later about how much she gave to me.

During the latter part of that time I did come back and dip my toe into the water of this incarnation, this lady Anthea whom I had known and worked with occasionally in that life. By this stage, I recognised that we had made this agreement when we were both still upstairs and I hoped that I still had enough integrity to honour that. Even though I didn't like the idea of living in a female, I did agree to this and I must honour that agreement which is obviously what I have done.

So, I did keep coming to visit her and then returning to Mark's body. Because I was in London and she was in Melbourne the time differences made that very easy. I could legitimately leave during my night times. As Mark's body deteriorated so he was sleeping more and I had more opportunity. I must have come heaps of times.

Eventually, I decided I had to honour this prior agreement and commitment. As Saint-Germaine has said, after Mark's life had physically ended, I had to do my review which was why it took so long to come and be fully integrated. It probably took twelve months after Mark's death to be comfortable. I was still a little bit edgy thinking that I now have another thirty years or so living in this female body. It took me a long time to get totally settled with this situation.

Anyway, her soul and mine have now integrated, melded and we are one. I am happily along for the ride now. I am happily experiencing these interesting things. I was aware of channelling in my life as Mark I had some interest in it then but to now have this experience has been quite amazing. Now that I am integrated and settled I'm grateful for this unexpected opportunity.

All the other things she does – she is left-brained enough which was partly what appealed when I was Mark she still has all those qualities and now more so. As Saint-Germaine explained, my intellect has enhanced hers which is now often the source of coming up with these inspirational moments she has been having increasingly and not just in the context of this work. I have enjoyed that.

Her self-confidence has been enhanced enormously. As Mark, I was not only strong but very self-confident, perhaps too much so sometimes. When I think back on it perhaps I didn't need to be quite as arrogant as I was sometimes, but that is irrelevant now. So her self-confidence and willingness to speak out about this channelling work has increased and she has much more confidence in standing up in potentially very difficult situations and declaring her hand. I am really pleased that I have been able to contribute these strengths to her in particular.

I now do what any incarnated soul does and that is, follow the day-to-day ups and downs. For me, one of the things I did not particularly experience in that life was the ongoing health issues that have plagued her for the last two or three years. So from my soul's perspective that has been a counterbalance to my life then. Leaving aside my last nine months where I just deteriorated, the rest of my life was very healthy. So this incarnation has fulfilled a balancing need for those experiences, which is a bonus for me although it is an ongoing concern for her. I know that she is aware that as she ages, this may or may not get any better.

I can't think of anything else. In the future, I am unlikely to come out again because it is rather complicated when I am melded with her soul. It's a very odd feeling channelling back through her own physical body in which we normally live every day. I would rather not come and do this unless there is a genuine need. So on that note, I will say good-bye.

Saint-Germaine

That was fascinating to watch and hear. That's not something I have ever seen before where the physical's own soul plus a walk-in comes back through channelling. That's convoluted. Nevertheless, I'm sure we are all grateful to Mark for making that effort. It was a weird effort. The whole situation was never set up for that to happen.

Moving on, Mary was another incarnation that the soul we know as Anthea experienced around two thousand years ago. What I'm saying is that this was a single soul that we will call Anthea-Mary for this discussion.

> Now Mary is still up here; she is not a walk-in. The question is – how can Anthea have been Mary if, in reverse, Mary is still sitting up here when Anthea is incarnate down there? If it's one soul then how come it has split (if that's the word) into Anthea, incarnate now and Mary, still upstairs?
>
> It certainly is a reincarnation but the question is – of which and who and what? (I'm trying to find the words.) The Anthea-Mary soul did that life as Mary but this time Anthea has come back separate from Mary and that in part was because Anthea agreed to have her soul enhanced by Mark. This is getting complicated; let me explain.
>
> Anthea has done these first sixty-odd years with, not a different soul but a part of that Anthea-Mary soul which has come back as Anthea. This has then been added to by the Mark soul for the experience of this particular incarnation. But a lot of Anthea-Mary is still sitting up here, separately for the moment, as Mary.

What will happen when Anthea passes is that Mark will separate out and go back to being Mark or whatever he's going to do. Anthea will go back to Mary and that will become an integrated soul-unit again, the Anthea-Mary soul.

Souls choose to do this splitting for a number of reasons including coming back as identical twins. If they're going to do a joint venture with a walk-in then they might feel they don't need all of that soul because it is going to be added to, complemented by, the walk-in.

It's also possible that Mary came in full and lived as Anthea up until the point where Mark was getting ready to move in when part of her then moved out. That's also possible. It's all this fluidity. I know in human terms, things have discrete boundaries. A brick is a brick is a brick and even if it's broken, it's still a brick. But this is all fluid. If you think of rivers running into the sea, you couldn't ever say that any particular drop of water was the river and this other drop was the sea. It all just blends and melds. Souls are like that.

How many people have a walk-in?

Very few. A lot of people, probably the majority, would do a life, go back, and then come back in due course to do another one. It would be straightforward. But reincarnation is not always cut and dried. These are complicated scenarios because very few people have the need to do a walk-in.

Up until recent times, walk-ins were very rare. But it's becoming more common often for the reasons that Tobias and Ben both said, "I don't want to do all this early stuff again. I've done enough of the early difficulties in previous lives."

Can there be a walk-out?

Can there be a walk-out through the soul's choice and before the physical death of the human? There must be criteria – you can't just say, "I don't like this and I want to come home to mummy." That's not acceptable. There must be very strong and very clear criteria. If human free-will leads the physical boy, man, down a path which is so far adrift from its soul plan and there's nothing to be gained from it staying, then in general terms I would have thought it possible.

But regardless, every human always has a soul for the whole its physical life, which implies that one of the two souls involved in a walk-in must stay until death.

Chapter 7
PAST LIVES

Where are past life memories stored, in the physical or the soul or both?

Good question and the answer is probably both. When the soul first incarnates these certainly come in with it, so initially they are stored in the soul where they stay. When the physical dies, the soul takes all that back plus the experiences from this incarnation to add to its collection of lives.

However, research on the physical brain[6] has shown that if you put electronic probes onto the temporal lobe of the brain itself, ie not the skull, then the patient will recall a past life or lives. So that part of the brain is either a storage mechanism or there is some connection between it and the soul's storage. Now I have no clue whether it is one or the other. The researcher's conclusion was that the memories are stored in

---

[6] Wilder Penfield, 1891-1976, Canadian neurosurgeon.

that part of the brain but he was coming from a left-brained, scientific paradigm which leaves no room for a soul anyway.

Have you had past lives with people you are close to in this life?
The logical answer is sometimes yes and sometimes no. When you have that thundering 'standing in the doorway and falling in love' experience (to quote one of Anthea's friends) that instant jaw-dropping recognition, that is what's happening; one soul is recognising the other. This is virtually always a person you've never seen or met before and it's definitely a recognition of a soul you have shared a past life or lives with, probably in a close and loving relationship of whatever sort. Now that could still be siblings; it doesn't have to have been partners. Both souls are recognising that close, important, loving connection from the past. Then suddenly *bing*, it's back again, like a bolt of lightning across the room.

Close friends and close family members are similar although here the answer could be no. If you haven't previously shared any close, long-standing friendships, this time you might have chosen that close bond as a new experience from the other point of view. There are people in their fifties and sixties who are still friends with childhood mates, ie very long-standing and close friendships.

People who you have affairs with are even more likely to have shared your past lives. You often have affairs with them because you couldn't marry them or they weren't around at the time or they have come into your life later on. This is where the affair is of the heart and not just of lust. With in-love affairs, there is an old, very strong connection from past lives. It's quite common actually.

People you marry – sometimes yes and sometimes no, for all the same sorts of reasons. You might marry someone you've not had a past life with because you want a close relationship because you've not experienced that before, let's say. You might have been a single person in many of your lives and now you want to experience the closeness, the mutual support and the sharing of everything that goes into a marriage. Other times, long-standing, really good marriages will often be past-life relationships of some sort, again not necessarily as partners. It's a mixture of everything.

Do our passions come from past lives and if so why are we repeating them?

Yes, they do. We can be almost categoric about that. So why would we bring them forward? Two reasons come to mind.

Let's say they have been a passion in the past and you might bring that forward to use as a strength to help you towards your goal for this life. As you will read, Ben said that he was going to bring forward his experience of a cross-cultural marriage as a strength to help him this time. But how Anthea's passion for port [wine] has carried forward to serve her in this life, I have yet to observe. But there's no question that she's passionate about it.

The other side of the coin is that you have been passionate about it before but you have failed to achieve some goal around that passion, so you bring it forward to try and achieve it again. To illustrate:

> With Anthea's port passion, there was a life in the 1870s along the Douro River in Portugal where she (as a man) and her brother had a vineyard on very steep slopes. When the phylloxera bug[7] came along they were completely wiped out along with many, many others. The vineyards in that area were decimated and

---

[7] Phylloxera is an insect which feeds on the roots of vines eventually killing them. Towards the end of the 19th century, this bug devastated vineyards all over the world.

they had no source of income. They were two unmarried brothers, a karmic pair very likely, so they went to the city because that was the only place they could get work to put bread on the table. They never really talked about what they saw as a failure.

Certainly, it was a physical failure because the vineyard was wiped out, but it was not a failure because of anything they did. There was nothing they could have done. Today you understand how this bug works but back then nobody did.

Now in soul terms that could be why she's carried it forward this time; because it was unfulfilled (better word) not a failure. Until that pest came along, the vineyard was doing very well and they were happy working at what they loved. It was all good. But it might have carried forward because it was unfinished or unfulfilled.

Do favourite pieces of music reflect past lives in some way?

Often, but not always. If you hear a piece of music for the first time and it goes *dong*, resonates with you, that is very, very likely to be a connection or a bridge to some past-life person or situation. It doesn't necessarily mean that you composed that piece of music in a past life. You might have lived with someone who was a classical pianist in any era, and they would practice all the time so you would hear it. You might have been married to them. There can be different reasons. To illustrate:

Anthea first heard Beethoven's *Für Elise* when she was thirteen. It instantly resonated and continues to this day to make the hairs on the back of her neck stand up. At that age, she had never heard of past lives of course.

She eventually learnt that she had been Beethoven's valet so she lived with the man and heard his music all the time. That particular piece was very poignant and still is because it was written just after the only lady he ever proposed marriage to, had declined him.

If you slowly get to like a piece of music, it's much less likely to be a past-life connection. Anthea has slowly evolved a liking for the very modern and minimalist music of Philip Glass. Because it is so modern there can be no past-life equivalent, and whatever Philip Glass has done in his past lives, it's extremely unlikely to include composing that style of music. So that is an acquired learning in this life.

It can be both and everything else in between. Take nursery rhymes. Earlier generations grew up teaching their children nursery rhymes. They're not particularly past-life connections; they are a societal thing that gets handed down from one generation to the next. You resonate with them because you've heard them ever since you were a wee toddler.

How do past-life connections with physical places manifest? Is déjà vu a connection from a past life?

In this day and age, you have four mechanisms for seeing places outside your own area or country: books, television, the internet and physical travel. You are more likely to explore the internet, books or television programs before you spend money to get on a plane to go to a remote and obscure culture like Tibet, for instance. If you see images of a place and your reaction is that instant, intuitive, "Wow! I'd love to visit that," then that very likely indicates a past life or lives in that place, or, that culture but not that place. But if you are reacting to the images of a particular place then it's much more likely to have been that actual place. To illustrate:

> In the early 1980s, long before she was into any of this spiritual stuff, Anthea went to China. Preparation for this trip was largely from travel brochures and a travel guidebook, all with images of the Terracotta Warriors. On the day of the visit to the Warriors she just knew, a deep-down gut knowing, that she had to spend as much time as possible there. It was like a magnet; she just knew she had to be there. She had no clue why. She stood at the top of the first pit and couldn't get enough of it.
>
> She has been back two or three times since and every time it's that same incredibly strong, magnetic attraction. She knows now that she had a past life as one of the slaves who carved the Terracotta Warriors. This was in 200BC and more, and she spent that whole life working on these figures, living in nearby quarters with her fellow slaves who also carved these statues.
>
> Planning this holiday, she also wanted to include a trip on the Yangtze River but decided that she couldn't afford that additional cost. Even then, thirty-plus years ago, something deep inside her was saying there is a pull to the Yangtze even though there was no conscious understanding of what that driver was. There have also been past lives along that river. She did one life as a man enduring a very hard, subsistence life on the Yangtze. But that longing manifest years and years before she ever knew about that life.

Déjà vu is also about places. It will largely manifest from a place rather than a person. If you have an instant recognition of a person – irrespective of whether you fall in love with them – that manifests as this *oh-my-god* gut reaction, it's likely to be a past life. If you have a recognition of a place, especially if it's a fleeting, 'good grief, I've been here before,' it's more likely to be a déjà vu of that place. You might be passing through on a train for instance so you only get a fleeting glimpse. Even if you're standing in a place for much longer, not many places are the same as they were two hundred years ago never mind two thousand, so it can only be some tiny aspect that will trigger that memory. Because it's only a tiny physical trigger, it will be but a fleeting experience. It's almost always a connection to a past life. It's very unlikely to be a recognition of a place you visited forty or fifty years ago in this life.

Do our phobias result from past life experiences?

Phobias, oh my gawd. Almost definitely, almost every time. Snakes – *ugh!* Definitely. Many people have phobias about snakes, about heights or enclosed spaces and all of these absolutely come from past-life experiences which are not necessarily bad experiences. To illustrate:

> Anthea had a life about 2000-odd years ago in northern China or Mongolia where she was a snake-keeper. The society was such that they had snake pits for gaming and entertainment – it's too ghastly to even think about. But somebody had to look after these snakes and she was good with them. She knew how to manage them and she knew about anti-venom treatments.
>
> In this life, she freaks out about snakes and you have to ask why when that's a totally opposite reaction. But that's the whole point. This time she's come back to

be afraid because then she was totally comfortable with them. This life is to experience the opposite.

Phobias can be like that. You might be very scared of an enclosed space. Let's say you were buried alive in a past life. In this life, you might carry that forward because you absolutely do not wish to repeat that experience. So you will go out of your way to avoid the possibility by not getting into any enclosed space. The other possibility is that in this life you will embrace enclosed spaces because you are not afraid of them this time. Both are opposite perspectives. It can be for all those balancing-type reasons.

Being afraid of heights is the same thing. Maybe in a past life, you were really good at heights but in this life, you might want to experience the fear. Maybe in a past life, you wanted to overcome a fear of heights but you failed so you carry that back as a lesson to try and have another go at this time.

Do birthmarks and freckles or other skin marks come from past life injuries?
Yes, is the short answer, no question. To illustrate:

> Anthea's sister has a large birthmark on the outside of one knee. That was a big injury that took her leg off in a past life when she was a man in a war zone. In this life, the mark and the knee joint don't bother her at all.

Freckles and birthmarks, on the whole, don't bother people – with the modern exception being that when you expose them to enormous amounts of hot sun there is a chance of them becoming cancerous.

Anthea has lots of freckles of varying sizes, many of them in pairs. What are the pairs –bites from a two-pronged snake's fangs! Because she knew all about anti-venoms she never died from a snake bite in that life. So yes, they all have a meaning.

How else do past-life memories manifest in the human?

We've covered a lot of them in people and music and relationships. Now food is something we haven't talked about. These days many societies are very multi-cultural which means that you have access to foods that eighty or a hundred years ago you could not have even conceived of. Most commonly occurring early on in Western societies were foods of Chinese origin and more latterly foods of Indian origin and these days a much wider range too.

Let's say that when you were a teenager, you were taken to a Chinese restaurant and your reaction was, "Wow! I could eat this all day." When there is that instant connection in your gut, you can take that as a fairly strong indication of a past life or lives link to a Chinese culture. Now, this may not have been in China; it might have been for instance, on the gold-fields of California around the 1850s where many Chinese were working.

There's also the societal, human learning too. If you go to Chinese restaurant enough times you might learn to particularly like certain foods. But if there's that instant, wow, intuitive, I-*love*-this reaction, then it's likely to indicate a past life. To illustrate:

> A fabulous example is Anthea's friend Jan who is besotted by everything Chinese. She cooks Chinese food, she knows where all the dumpling restaurants are, she's been to China under the direst of circumstances and enjoyed and learnt. Under hugely

bad ill-health conditions she is still going to Chinese language classes to keep her skills up. There is no reason in her white, Anglo, Catholic upbringing in this life to have that depth of passion about the food, the language, the place, the people, everything.

This is a screamingly obvious example of many past lives in China under all sorts of circumstances. You have to ask, if she has had so many, why would she carry such a strong passion forward to this life?

In her case, she needed to live in a non-Chinese culture as a balance. She enjoyed all these past lives in China and they were very successful. In this life, she is a single lady of the Catholic faith in a white, Anglo culture and with a multitude of health issues. All of that is a composite of complete opposites which you can understand is a balancing experience.

So to summarise if there is anything, a book, a piece of fabric, a flower, whatever, that generates that instant, wow, gut-sinking feeling, that is an acid test that it's extremely likely to have come from a past-life experience.

Can emotions be triggered by past lives?

No, not directly. Emotional reactions to a past-life connection is a human response. That instant gut reaction is the recognition but the emotional response to that is a human thing and that is true whether it's a pleasurable reaction or a threatening one.

Can specific subjects trigger a past life recognition?

Recently there was a TV program about an extremely well-known personal trainer. Let's call her Denise. To illustrate:

> Denise has a long-standing, really strong passion for physical wellbeing, exercise and training. This probably originated in school because this would have been her first opportunity to learn this. Now these thirty or whatever years later, she is still as passionate about it as she ever was. This has to have come from past lives where she saw the benefit of exercise in keeping people healthy.
>
> Now that doesn't necessarily mean that in a past life she was also doing exercise to the same extent. She might have been in an environment where others around her were. In theory, she might have been a monk in the Shaolin Monastery in China where they still practice extreme martial arts, ie this would have been a life very much dedicated to physical wellbeing as part of their ethos. As a monk, she would have had contact with the outside community and could see that the locals of a similar age who were not exercising to the same extent, did not look as good. So she sees the benefit and carries it forward to deliver it in this life.

A past-life experience might carry forward as a benefit, something you were either good at or saw the advantage of, to use as a tool to help you achieve your goals in this life. It doesn't have to necessarily be a passion in a past life but it has to have been a very positive experience to carry it forward.

Now you could say – what about a very negative experience in a past life? To illustrate:

In a past life, Shirley was female and abused as a child by someone close to her. This time she's come back as a female again but is very strongly anti-men for no apparent reason. She's physically and mentally tough and in control, ie she manifests a lot of male qualities. She works in a male world, she is very outspoken and she certainly does not suffer fools gladly, because in this life she's saying, "I'm not having any man muck with me again." She's not saying this even subconsciously, but that quality could have carried forward into this life.

Do our commonly used phrases come from past-life experiences?

I think the answer is mostly yes although I am struggling to find the words to express it properly. The verbal expression itself is not directly from the soul. Let's use the fairly common phrase, 'the pain is killing me.' That phrase is likely to have come from a past-life experience. Now the soul is not doing a light-bulb, bing moment to put that phrase into the human's head, but it filters through the physical in some fashion. It's like a burrowing, a subconscious burrowing, so when that person suddenly experiences unexpected pain, that's going to be their automatic, intuitive reaction. Indirectly it has come from the soul.

A phrase like 'oh my god!' when something totally amazing or unexpected happens can be directly from the soul. Not just for bad things like car accidents but also for something really wonderful like you win the lottery, then it's 'Oh, My host soul!' It's the same sort of mechanism as those light-bulb moments of inspiration albeit with a different outcome. If a phrase is used relatively frequently, it's likely to have come from the soul via this burrowing mechanism. To illustrate:

As a mature adult, for some years Susan had used the phrase, "I'm invisible" in the context of perceiving that she didn't have many friends. She underwent a past-life regression in which she saw herself as a female in a warring Maori tribe in New Zealand in the 1800s. In order to escape the fighting, she was forced to hide in densely wooded forest until the fighting was over.

After the session ended, it was explained to her that in order to survive in that life, she had to be invisible. She has not used the phrase since.

In your Western world, particularly through the advent of the internet and texting, new phrases come along all the time. In the 1950s and '60s, you would have had phrases to indicate that something was nice or acceptable. These days young people will say that something is cool. Now that's a word that has developed in society. An older adult who still wishes to be seen as socially acceptable might start using it for those reasons. So phrases like that are not soul generated, but if it's an instinctive, gut-reaction phrase, then very likely it will be.

What is happening when suddenly out of the blue, you hear somebody you know unexpectedly utter a phrase that you use but very few other people do?

That is also very likely to be a past-life connection which is manifesting via the same burrowing mechanism. The other person's soul has recognised yours in the sense that you have both shared a past life or lives but perhaps that life wasn't so intense. It was still good or you wouldn't want to recognise them again. It was probably long and happy but not intensely, deeply connected in the way that close couples are, or not passionately in love.

Whatever this phrase is, it's likely to be a modern-day one. The soul is sending out a signal and using this phrase as a mechanism to say to the other human that there is this connection. When the first person says it, the other person will recognise and register it.

That's one example of a whole less-intense level of sending a signal to past-lives connections. Somebody says that I've always liked that piece of obscure music and you too have always liked it; things where you overlap in liking something. Not things like the men in the pub really liking a particular beer, more intuitive things.

This can also apply to negative reactions. The two souls will recognise each other and that they were involved in a less-than-satisfactory situation in the past. This was not necessarily something as radical as one killing the other, but something that was unfinished or unfulfilled or some disappointment that has been left behind. These will trigger less strong reactions but if there are enough of these coincidences, the sensitive person will be aware of them and realise that there is some sort of past-life connecting going to some lesser degree. But you would only be aware if you're alert to this coincidence because it's not a slap-across-the-jaw type wallop. It's much more subtle and gentle but it's still that signal being sent.

What is happening when you get goosebumps all over or an involuntary shiver down the spine or you feel like somebody has walked over your grave?

This is a past life connection. When a soul you have shared a past life with is still discarnate up here, is recognising a situation or circumstances which are enough to bring back the memory from that previous life (or lives) and both souls are going *ding*, "I remember," which is why you get this much stronger reaction. It might be more than just one soul; it might be two or three all of whom have shared that past experience. This is particularly likely if these souls were also a karmic group in that past life.

But these souls are still upstairs and you are incarnate. When they recognise this situation, they resonate with it as do you, which is why you feel this strong physical, electrical-type reaction like the hairs on the back of your neck standing up. And that's why it's a much stronger reaction than if you just resonate to say a piece of music. The goosebumps or whatever are the strongest of all the reactions you are likely to have to a past life connection.

What happens when you casually meet a person who you have had a past life experience with but that past connection was distant ie, someone, you were not close to?

I guess it depends on the strength of that past-life connection. If in that past life you were distant colleagues and didn't have much to do with each other, then in this life when you meet them there would not necessarily be a strong reaction. If it was a strong past-life connection then you will get some sort of reaction in this life albeit of varying strength. This would start with the goosebumps, through to recognising someone across a crowded room through to "oh maybe I have seen them before" right down to nothing at all. To illustrate:

> Many years ago, Anthea did a past-life weekend workshop with Denise Linn who was extremely knowledgeable about past lives and how they manifest. All the participants in that workshop were unknown to Anthea except the one friend she had gone with. Denise made the comment that "you will have all met each other somewhere at some time, in a past life which is why you are all here today". And she was right.
>
> Anthea did not react to any of them in any way beyond a human reaction. There was no resonance from a past life with any of these eighteen or twenty people. This

indicates that she would only have shared that past life or past lives in a casual or passing manner, ie not close and certainly not intimate in any way. They might have been a neighbour down the street who she would see periodically over many years but there would not have been any emotional attachment. She might have sat on the same train every morning for thirty years but you are not friends or emotionally connected. So it's very likely everyone is this class had had relationships like that.

Can you explain about energy seduction in a soul?

Souls are all energy as is everything up here. Everything on earth has its own unique energies. Just to explain, in nature one sort of grass will have its own energy which is a combination of frequencies. A different grass will have nearly similar frequencies. A tree is also a plant so it will have a different but nearby combination of frequencies. Animals, for instance, all the cat family, will have related frequencies but they will be different from say, insects or elephants. Same thing throughout the animal world.

Each individual human also has their own unique combination of frequencies. This is a large mixture because humans are very complex, physically, physiologically, electrically, emotionally, intellectually. Each of those items generates its own frequencies. Going back to the soul bubble, as we saw in Chapter 1 each component, ie each human trait, has its own frequency and that is what the soul energy bubble is made up from. So, therefore, each human is unique because its composite of frequencies from the components in its soul is unique.

Moving onto things that are manufactured in the human world, these also have a combination of frequencies. Let's take a simple example. If you are creating a bronze sculpture, the bronze is made from several metals each of which has a very specific frequency. So the sculpture ends up with the energies from its innate metals plus the energy that it has absorbed from the process of being sculpted. The end product ends up with its own unique combination of all these energies.

Everything on earth is in this situation. The more complicated the item, the more complex its frequencies. An aeroplane is a very sophisticated piece of machinery and its energies are hugely complex and interrelated.

As you will read, Ben was being seduced by the energy of technology. Computers will have a combination of frequencies and different electronic gadgets will have different combinations. They all have a large number of electronic and electrical components which creates a unifying effect, ie they all belong to the same family of electronic products.

That was what Ben was attracted to. If that attraction is strong enough, it becomes a seduction. If it becomes even stronger, it becomes an addiction which we don't particularly get into up here but in theory, that would be possible. If Ben couldn't stand back from it enough to see how it was affecting him, it has the potential for Ben to become addicted to that energy.

However, Ben appears to have overcome that seduction before he incarnated. Towards the end of his story, Gabriel was very clear that Ben had calmed down and came back to do his soul planning, all of which he achieved. We have to assume that the seduction will not carry forward. That's one level of seduction up here; you overcome it and it doesn't follow you, or if it does, you learn to manage it and not get re-seduced.

Going back to Jan, you have to ask why has this Chinese passion filtered through? I'm beginning to think that in her case, it's the seduction. The seductive energies from so many happy, successful, wonderful past lives in a Chinese culture and this time she was coming back to try not to be seduced back into it again. Being a strong Catholic is a very good way of trying to avoid that but largely this has failed – and that's not to say that this is good or bad, but the seduction seeped in quite early on and she's never been able to resist. This is a human thing. The soul has come in with the purpose of trying to achieve that goal but because of human free-will, it has failed.

Mark is another example of how the seduction can happen because of human circumstances.

> After a past life where he was actively engaged in religion, Mark reincarnated with a goal to live a secular life as a balance. Mark's parents divorced when he was in his mid-teens leaving him to fend for himself both financially and emotionally. He lodged with a family, who were active church-goers, and quickly discovered that the church provided the care and support that was lost after his parents separated. That's a very human reason for engaging with the energy of the church. His human needs were sufficiently great that his free-will took that on board, absorbed it and lost sight of the soul's need to live a secular life.

Fred and Anthea were friends in this life and Fred's story is yet another example of energy seduction:

> Fred and Anthea have shared a number of past lives in European Catholic monasteries, hundreds of years ago. As part of his soul planning process, Fred promised and avowed to avoid the seduction of that Catholic-church energy in this coming life.
>
> He grew up in the Catholic faith. He chose that particular family to taste it and then to try to be strong

enough to leave it behind, but as an adult, his free-will choice was to carry on with that faith. In other words, in his twenties, he failed. Through all his adulthood and secular working life, he was an active member of the church. Once he retired, the family had left home and work was no longer, he succumbed to the big part of the seduction and decided to become ordained. So he has failed badly.

Can you tell us about past life connections where they manifest as a big negative wallop rather than the OMG-positive ones?

Things that hit you so hard that you react with instant, uncontrollable, gut-wrenching sobs from the pit of your stomach are also a reaction to a past-life event or place or person or circumstance. Two things are possible: in that past life or lives, something really bad happened around the circumstances that trigger the reaction, or, something that you really wanted to achieve was left unfinished or unfulfilled. In this life, an event happens which then triggers this human reaction of tears from the bottom of your heart which leaves you feeling numb, confused and totally wiped out. It can be a regret or a sadness or perhaps a big disappointment that you've been let down somehow. Going back to Fred, to illustrate:

> When Fred told Anthea that "I'm going to turn my collar round," her gut reaction instantly kicked in with the sinking of the stomach. It was like a sense of abandonment. Not long later she wrote to him saying that it felt like, "God-1, Gentiles-0." Well, God did win, didn't he! She was absolutely gutted. The seduction was too strong; he just couldn't resist and withstand it.

On the day of his ordination, she was living about ninety miles away but she just knew, deep down, that despite the distance she had to be the service. From the minute she stepped into that pew, the tears poured, embarrassingly so. There was no way she could find the tap, never mind turn it off. It was an outpouring of abandonment and grief and loss that he'd gone to the extreme of not remembering or not honouring this vow.

Past-life regression

A past-life regression is a technique that uses hypnosis or a deep trance-like state to recover hidden memories and images of past lives or incarnations. Under hypnosis, you are guided by the practitioner through the events that you see to reveal the details of this life or lives. These sessions should only be undertaken with a trained hypnotherapist or past-life regressionist; the practitioner can be both of course. If you only ever do this once or twice you are likely to see those lives that will help you most in this life.

Can past-life regressions help our health?

If humans have lingering health issues where the painful area has a birthmark or mole or lots of freckles over it, then I would strongly suggest, and I mean strongly, that undergoing a past-life regression where that health issue is addressed, will help resolve the problem.

There is plenty of anecdotal evidence to demonstrate this and to illustrate this is a real-life story from Danielle, a professional past-life regressionist. This one is about physical pain:

Claire had complained of pain in her right knee for years and after much resistance, she accepted that it was arthritis because there was no other explanation. She had a regression where she saw a life in which she was a servant who spent many hours on her knees scrubbing floors. When she tripped and fell badly on her knee it never healed cleanly because the hours spent on her knees scrubbing interrupted the healing process. Once Claire knew the reason, her knee pain disappeared.

Just as in this example, if a residual memory from a past-life injury is causing the pain, then a past-life regression where you saw what happened in that life, has a very good chance of helping relieve and release that pain. However, if there is genuine physical damage like arthritis for instance, then I can't say that a past-life regression would help.

The other things are mental and emotional issues. If there is an ongoing issue about say, lack of confidence and you have failed to resolve this through conventional counselling and therapy, then you have to ask if a past-life regression would help? There is a good possibility of that as well.

Maybe in a past life, you were a slave who had to be subservient, or a child in Victorian times where children were seen and not heard and you grew up being almost invisible. That could be a big burden that you bring back into this life because this time you want to balance and release it. So this time you are lacking self-confidence and maybe live in your shell, only speaking when spoken to because that carries forward. A past-life regression which showed you that life as a Victorian-era child would help you to understand and to release it allowing you to be yourself and go forward much more confidently.

Another story from Danielle to illustrate:

> Emma was obsessed with binge eating and lacked the motivation to exercise. She regressed to a life in England about a hundred years ago where she was a young boy aged about six who lived with a younger brother and his mother.
>
> The father had fled and they were destitute, living in an abandoned house where they literally nearly froze during the winter. They scavenged for food which was usually rotten. He had no energy to do anything because there was nothing fuelling his body. When the mother died, the boy had to take care of both of them.
>
> Once Emma became aware of this, the binge eating ceased and she became a cross-fit champion. Today she can't get enough of exercising. This happened within three months of doing the regression.

How do we remember past lives? Can we believe that the earlier ones we see are 'the truth' when we have experienced subsequent ones which might colour that recall?

That's a really curly question and I have to say, very deep and very subtle. The answer must be yes and no. In a general sense, the whole purpose of having more incarnations is to learn more things and the memories from each life are cumulative. I'm going to use John the Baptist to illustrate:

> John was a significant single man in that life. The experiences that he accumulated from his life as John the Baptist he carried in his soul when he passed and those learnings and memories stay with him forever.

Let's just say he comes back later on as an ordinary mother – in reality, I have no idea. She raises the kids and looks after home and hubby and the family, and it was a good life. He suddenly has a whole bunch of new experiences from the other side of the coin: he's female, he's married and he has children, all three are the total opposite of the John-the-Baptist life. So his cumulative learnings and memories are added to.

That can repeat many times and the lives are often going to be opposites so that the soul can experience the other perspective. If a soul has not learnt as much as it could in a particular life, it will come back to repeat the opportunities for those learnings again.

Next, we have to say – what is the truth? The truth is subjective. If two people share an experience, the truth from either person's perspective will be subtly different because you're both seeing it from a different point of view. When you might say the sky is blue, an alien might say it's green. Even things that you might call facts can be subjective.

Leaving aside the philosophy around what is truth, the question then comes down to – how can a soul remember, in such detail, lives that happened two thousand years ago, which in your human terms is an extremely long time. Plenty of humans struggle to remember what they had for dinner yesterday.

Firstly, the remembering process up here is a lot easier, a lot clearer and a lot simpler than it is in human terms. Each life is stored in a separate, self-contained bucket so that the details of that life are not intermingled with other lives. Any soul can dip into any particular bucket in his memory and consciousness, and this bucket over here will be that life, two thousand years ago, as John the Baptist. This separate bucket somewhere else alongside will be the life he then lived several hundred years later as a wife and mother, so in terms of remembering, he just has to dip into the applicable bucket. Even though this subsequent life will have added to his collective learnings and memories, it should not affect how he recalls and retells the story of the John-the-Baptist life.

That's how it works for any soul recalling any life. They think about and focus on telling the story which should be as close to the truth as anyone can give, and to be fair, as close to the truth as their memories can give back to them. That's a limitation that happens to every human being on the earth-plane. If you ask an eighty-year-old what they did last week, they will give you a vague answer, but if you ask them what they did sixty years ago they will give you a crystal-clear answer. It's all about the vagaries of how the physical and mental processes work in a human, some of which colour the memories you take back with you, if not to the same degree.

If you are doing a past-life regression, the stories that you see are as close to the truth as you're ever going to get given those limitations of memory and recall.

OK, enough from me. After all this theory and talk about souls returning, this seems like a good place for me to hand over to Ben and let him tell the actual story of planning his next life…

Chapter 8
BEN'S JOURNAL

One day in September 2013, we were doing a channelling session (for a different book) when a male-energy soul came through. He announced himself as Ben and explained that he hadn't been on earth for around two thousand years.

He asked if we would explain computers to him. We were a bit surprised but said we'd be happy to. He said that there were souls up there who had returned recently who talked about computers but he didn't understand. He felt an outsider because it was so far removed from his own experiences. He also said, "There are any number of us up here [in spirit] who have had a gap of this length [two thousand years] between incarnations and even longer. It's not uncommon."

At the end of that session Saint-Germaine suddenly popped up, "Aha, I wonder if he is preparing for a new incarnation."

Now there's a thought…

At our next session, Ben returned. We explained the internet, emails and social media to him. He asked questions and eventually seemed satisfied.

He then asked if we had any questions for him. Unprepared, we said no. However, in the week that followed, I realised that we'd missed a glorious opportunity to ask if he was thinking about a new life. So we agreed that if he reappeared we would ask.

What follows is Ben's story. This is shown as journal entries for although the majority of entries are from Ben, occasionally other speakers also added their perspectives.

Planning

Ben   13 September 2013

I heard you asking about the process of planning for a new incarnation. I thought, oh, that's interesting. Maybe it would be helpful to human understanding if we were to document this in some way. I know there are enough people with what you call spiritual and new-age interests (for lack of a better phrase) who would probably be extremely interested to hear a first-hand example of how this works.

I've thought about this and I'm happy to give you updates periodically when I have something to report. I will tell you a little bit now about what we've done so far.

There's no point me using words like recently simply because my 'recently' is very different from yours. At some point not so far back, I got it into my head that I would like to come back to experience all these new things, particularly the technology that has evolved so enormously. The driver for that development was probably the two world wars but particularly the Second World War. As you know the first computer came out of those circumstances. Technology has grown exponentially over the last eighty or a hundred years. We have young souls up here who talk about computers and lots of other things I don't understand. I thought that I would like to come and experience some of that, just to see what on earth it's all about (pardon the pun!).

I thought now why do I want to do this? What do I want to learn from this? I don't want to come just to learn how to drive a computer. The technology has to be the vehicle for whatever my soul needs to learn from this next incarnation.

The original temptation to incarnate has come from curiosity and wanting to interact with this technology. However, in our terms, that is not enough reason to come back. There has to be a bigger reason to do with the development of my own or somebody else's soul. At the moment that's the point I'm working on, trying to understand what I need to learn… what I could use the technology as the vehicle for learning and experiencing beyond the technology itself.

We have groups of angels whose role it is to guide and counsel souls who are considering incarnation. It's part of the planning and preparation. I've been allocated a group of these good folk and when I have enough questions I will seek a meeting with them.

Sometimes Daniel[8] comes to join because he has wisdom that I don't. The group will say, "have you thought about this aspect?" or "have you thought about…?". They try to guide my thinking. But the decision-making is always and only mine. If I come up with some decision which, from their perspective, sounds so crazy that it's going to be detrimental, they would try to gently guide me away from that idea. I would have the wit to listen and listen hard, take it on board and then re-evaluate. It may be that even after re-consideration I still decide I want to do some of it. They would always respect that and I would probably have to, not justify but explain why I'm still thinking that way. In time, between us, we would evolve and resolve that conundrum because that's what it is.

At the moment we're looking at two or three years out from now in your human terms and at this early point in the planning, it's likely to be a walk-in. In a way that's being a bit selfish, although I'm not sure that selfish is a concept that a soul has because everything it needs to do, is for itself anyway. Beyond that, I don't yet have any idea about my soul's purpose or the circumstances and nature of the physical body, not even male or female.

---

[8] A soul who shared Ben's last life as his father.

Daniel   13 September 2013

Ben is going to come back to earth. It's exciting for me to see how he will get on and to help him plan this grand adventure and see what and who he chooses to come back as and under what circumstances. I have no control over it. He comes and asks things periodically. He's keen to experience some of this. We've all got things to learn and that's his next big undertaking. He might choose to be one of the starving millions in Africa or an Eskimo, who knows…

Planning team

Ben   23 September 2013

Who are these angels and guides that you mentioned?

They're saying that they don't particularly want to go down this path; it's not really relevant who they are. Even if I were to tell you it would only beg heaps more questions about the structure of angels and guides and all the other folk up here, all of which gets way outside the process for an individual planning his incarnation. A group of mentors (is a really good word) will be allocated to guide you, anyone, through the planning process and be there for you when you have questions.

Did we have guides allocated to us before we came back?
Yep. Any individual, any soul, could spend years and years, twenty, thirty, fifty years, planning if that's what it needed. These good souls, these mentor-guides would always be around if you had questions. As you got closer to the time of coming back you would probably have more get-togethers more often. There's an awful lot of planning and meetings to be had to iron out every minute detail, as I'm sure I'm going

to learn. Once they're allocated, they are there for you for however long it takes. That's their purpose and role up here for eternity.

Will they be mentors just for you or will they be working with others too?

Gosh, yes. Any group of guides, angels, spirits would specialise in mentoring say, souls which had come back as young people. Or souls which had returned through war-torn trauma, for instance. These two groups would have had very different human experiences and therefore different needs up here now, so the answer is yes. You would call them specialist teams I suppose.

Up here, I'm seen as a young person, part in energy and part in what I'm trying to do and connect with here, hence my interest in computers. My team are specialists in helping young adults who wish to come back. They will be with me until I physically reincarnate. At the same time, they will also be guiding other souls as well.

Terminology

Saint-Germaine   23 September 2013

I need to clarify here about these phrases old and young souls in the way Ben is using them. Right at the start, we said that Ben is an old soul which is correct when you understand it by the definition I gave earlier [see Chapter 1]. Now we have both Ben and Daniel saying he is a young soul, so what is going on? How can he be young if his last life was two thousand years ago or more?

The best analogy I can give is that of a character in a play in your theatres and films. Let's say a man of thirty is acting the character of an eighteen-year-old male. In the play, this 'person' is always young, a teenager, despite the fact that in his personal life the actor might be a family man. But just before every performance, the actor has to 'become' the teenager and the age and mentality of his character.

Ben wants to return to experience computer technology which is largely the domain of young adult men. I think of people like Mark Gates, Steve Jobs or Mark Zuckerberg who as quite young men invented the amazing technologies that your computers are based on today. So already Ben is getting into character (I believe is your phrase) in the same way as the actor does for each performance.

Temptation of technology

Ben   16 April 2014

I thought I'd give you a bit of an update, in part triggered by Anthea's continuing involvement with this new little computer thing, a tablet I think. She's been using this while she's been away and I've been watching and puzzling over this, thinking this is new and different. I guess I have to try and get some understanding of this as well. I really am puzzled by it.

Now, have I got anything to add about my journey up here? Maybe a little. Time has moved on and I have pretty much made the final decision to come back to earth, so that's a step forward. I am ninety per cent committed to this path. Then you have to say – what has changed in my thinking in the six months since we last talked?

Partly her playing with this tablet has made me realise that the technology is just moving so fast. If I want to experience that, I have to come back pretty quickly because it will just keep progressing. I'm not fearful about missing out but my sense is that the longer I leave it, there'll be all this background, phases in this technology's evolution, that I will have missed.

Okay, I will have had some understanding from our conversations and from talking to young people up here who had use of this technology in their lives on earth except now they're up here and not using it anymore. My only direct contact is you two in terms of the next step of these technologies. While that's fine, it's still not the same as having first hand, hands-on experience. I'm realising that if this is really important to me, then I have to get my skates on and come back fairly soon.

This also reinforces what I hinted at earlier, that I would come back as a walk-in. In my evolutionary terms, it's okay that I skip all the early childhood basics this time. I might come back as a fourteen-year-old, something like that, maybe fifteen. Probably as a male. While the girls are good at the technology these days, it strikes me that it's really the young men who are more focused on it. I'm not being bigoted, that's just my observation from up here.

Now you might then ask – what do my guides think about that?

They're saying to me, that's all well and good but I still haven't identified the bigger, soul, reason for wanting to do this. I think I said before, wanting to play with and understand the technology is fine but in soul-evolutionary terms, it's not a good enough reason for reincarnating. I am still cogitating that.

I'll tell you what comes to mind: Adam and Eve. It's a bit like this technology is the temptation, the apple on the tree. I don't mean temptation in terms of evil but it's seductive, this energy of technology. I'm getting seduced by its amazing possibilities, but at least I recognise that is what's going on. I realise that I need to marry this interest – let's just call it an interest, I haven't been totally seduced yet – with a better soul purpose. But I haven't yet resolved that dilemma. On one hand, my head is saying, "You haven't come up with a good enough reason to reincarnate yet," and on the other hand, there's all this seduction with the technology going on. That sounds a bit daft but that's what it feels like to me.

Until I get my head around the bigger need, then I'm not going to be allowed (if that's the word). I can't just suddenly whip off and say, "Oye, George down the road, I'm coming in." It's got to be a bit more elegant and planned and mutually beneficial than that.

I have to find the young man. We have to make it okay with the soul that's already within that young man. We then have to work out all the details as well. There's still a lot to do before I can suddenly come and tap you on the shoulder in downtown Melbourne.

Would this be similar to what Tobias did?

Yes, that's my plan. Now Tobias… am I right that Tobias picked a lad of about eight or ten?

Twelve.

Okay, yes. I want to pick someone maybe older than that, with a more mature persona if you like. Maybe somebody about sixteen would be better. That's my thinking at the moment.

I know that a young man today is a very different person and in a different situation from my last life back then. I would feel more comfortable and get on better in a young man rather than a young woman. Too many other things going on for a sixteen-year-old girl. Prior experience and making this walk-in work quickly and efficiently is what I want. Therefore, going into something I know means I can adapt more quickly. My guides up here might tell me different but that's how I'm reading it at the moment.

I have made some progress. I've had more meetings with my guides and planning folk. That's included Daniel and Hannah[9] actually – female

---

[9] Hannah is a soul who was Ben's mother in his most recent past life.

energy guides are sometimes involved in this. Hannah is so full of common sense. Two thousand years ago, women didn't get a lot of credit for intelligence but Hannah had that rock-solid strength; she had common sense by the bucket-load which was just wonderful.

Those are the sorts of qualities I want to help me plan my next incarnation, so she's part of this too. I had to explain all this and ask if she could join. "Oh yes, that's fine; it's your planning process. If Hannah can help you and she's willing, then absolutely, why not."

I sense it's unusual to have too many of the folk you've done previous incarnations within the planning group but I was utterly clear that that was what I needed. There was no argument or discussion. Both Hannah and Daniel thought it was a bit of a privilege really and were pleased to be involved, which was lovely.

I think [Archangel] Gabriel is keeping a watchful eye on this planning process as well although he's not actively participating in the meetings. He would look out for me because I know he looked after me in that past life. But I get the sense there's more to it than I'm allowed to know at this stage. As always, Gabriel will tell us when he feels the time is right.

Purpose and goals

Ben   21 May 2014

So – have I made any headway with my soul purpose yet?

It's a double-edged sword really. I am seduced by the technology. We have the conversations and I understand a little more. Then Anthea says things like, "you need to think about hardware and software." I think oh! And I'm seduced a little further. Sucked in a little more about what there is to learn and the sweetness, as seduction always is, the sweetness of that thought. Then I go back and my guides all look at me in silence – nobody says anything. Nobody up here is judgemental; it's wonderful. But they all look and I say, "O…K. I know; it's not enough. I have to have a better reason."

"No, not better. You have to have a soul learning, experiential reason. Learning to play with computers is fun and fine but not enough."

"O…K. I know."

In all honesty, I have not yet resolved that issue but I have made some progress. In my last life, I married a lady, not of my culture, but both she and our child died. That was a huge trauma for me as anyone who has lost a child will know. But as part of my experience this time, I'm hoping to balance that by having a life where I can marry and have children who do survive because I feel that will be significant. You would probably say that makes some sense in terms of what you call karma. I would come back with an enhanced feeling for cross-cultural relationships even though in my day such relationships were virtually non-existent. It wasn't frowned on but because it happened so seldom, the individual would be taken for themselves and not judged because of their colour or background or parentage.

Those are both factors in what I think I need to do at a soul level for this incarnation. Because I also experienced a community-focused life last time, then if I can bring that back into this world even as a small contribution towards world, or even regional, peace then that would be karmically significant – and a huge step forward in terms of your planet's future. Your planet is in such a mess that you could start by bringing some peace to one place in the hope that it would be lasting only to find that it would be short-lived or that nearby peoples would invade as the Romans took over us.

I'm not arrogant enough to say that I'm coming to be the new modern messiah bringing world peace. That would be unbelievably egotistical and unrealistic. Once I'm in human form I have less control over how it will play out because human free-will becomes a fairly significant part of the decisions, actions and outcomes.

Maybe I've been a bit convoluted today but perhaps that explains a little about my soul reasons and my potential contributions.

Planning update

Ben   26 June 2014

We have definitely made some advances. We now have a timescale. Woo-hoo! And a more definite plan.

We have found a soul in a young man who is willing to share the space within this young man. Now, we need to give this life a name and I am going to call him Tom. I am mindful of Tobias; when he was coming back he called his young man Sam which is an American name – and let me say, my young man is not going to be in America. He's likely to be in an English-speaking part of the world, possibly Canada although I don't fancy the cold weather up there one jot, or Australia, possibly New Zealand. Both of those are much warmer and I might opt for those just on that basis alone. However, that's a minor detail.

We've found a person who's willing to share and Tom is aged around fourteen. Like Sam, he's also a bit of a loner, quiet but introspective and has a great intellectual capability that's not yet being used to anything like its capacity or his ability. He's coasting through school and curiously quiet about life. By that I mean he observes much and thinks about what he sees, about people's behaviour, particularly his colleagues and teachers. He's a single lad, I mean no siblings and unlikely to. His parents are older than you would expect from a fourteen-year-old. They had him later in life.

He's not aware that this event is likely to come to pass. We're in a broad agreement with his current soul, that we'll do this blending, melding, at some point. Probably two or three years hence. Tom's also curious and quite gifted about computers. Now that brings great opportunity but at the moment it scares me witless. I might come and ask more questions about computers.

That's all good and my guides up here are pleased that I've got to this point. They see it as a positive, concrete step rather than just wafting around and almost flirting with the idea that I might come back into the earth-plane again. It's not yet the point of no return but it's getting much closer to that irreversible commitment. I sense deep down that my guides must feel that I need to do this, not that they ever say, but I have to reach this point in my own time and in my own way of thinking. I'm much closer to accepting that I will actually, really and truly, come back and do a new incarnation.

Purpose

Ben   30 July 2014

What is your soul's purpose for this next incarnation?

I want to work out how to enhance the idea of peace using technology. How it can be used to maximise the spread of messages of peace, techniques for engendering peace, particularly across cultures that are so at odds with each other, to wit the Palestinians and the Israelis. That is so long-standing and so entrenched and both sides are right and both sides are wrong. Even sitting up here now, I can't see how that is ever going to get resolved.

My purpose is to try and work out how we can maximise current and future technology to somehow bring these warring parties to the table to talk and compromise and reach a peace agreement that will work for both of them. By that, I mean by not having things like the huge wall that currently divides Israel. In theory, that's one way of achieving peace but it's not peaceable. It is divisive and segregating. My concept is peace in the sense that I shake your hand, you are my brother across a different cultural divide but we can still live in neighbourly harmony.

That's my ideal. It's a big ask and I'm very aware of that – which in large part is what makes me still tentative about returning.

The planning is moving forward slowly. I still have some reluctance… I'm scared if I'm being truthful. I'm scared about the huge responsibilities. It's an enormous task to put on anyone's shoulders and I'm scared, in part, because of how little I understand of the technology. I know all of this stuff is learnable and it isn't hard. Clearly, if this is my soul purpose and plan, I would choose a walk-in to a young man who is already tuned into technology. There's no point starting out with a girl who's into frilly dolls and such like.

I'm conscious too that whatever I can learn here now will help but it will change so rapidly that it could be redundant before I ever get to a point of being able to use it.

What about the Canadian or Australian or New Zealander then?

This lad's parents look like moving. His father's profession is such that he could be in any of these countries and possibly all of them over time. Your global culture is far more mobile with the advent of air travel as well as electronically through the internet. At this point, it's where would they physically be when I did join? That is still unresolved. I have still chosen the same person and I'm pretty comfortable that it will work for him and for me but until it actually happens, it's not cast in concrete.

We're still doing progress meetings. Daniel and Hannah are less involved now. They were really helpful at the broad-brush, early planning stages with, "if this is what you want to do, then this is what you need to think about." Now we've moved onto the nitty-gritty detail they're interested but have less input. It's much more up to me and my guides to work out the detail.

Do you have timescales by which you have to make a commitment or decision?

No. It's when I feel comfortable doing it. I said earlier about four years. Four of your years is but a blink for us.

If you've picked out the lad who you would likely walk into and he's fourteen or so now…

He has to be that age to make it easier for him.

But if you didn't make that decision for another ten years let's say…

It would have to be a different person.

Commitment

Ben   22 October 2014

I'm making the most of this opportunity to come and tell you the good news. I have now irrevocably committed to returning to earth. Wow!

This has taken a lot… a *lot* of support from my team up here and a lot in my own head and heart to be totally convinced that this is what I need to do.

I am now past the point of no return and I will be back. I'm still committed to using technology and becoming a technical geek in order to try to progress or influence the idea of peace, somewhere in the world. I'm conscious that I need to not be totally seduced by the technology to the extent that I lose sight of the purpose of peace but that will be a human challenge which is easy enough to be aware of now.

My intent is still this same lad Tom, who is in New Zealand with his family. But there's an increasing chance that in the foreseeable future they will move to Canada. Now, this does not overly enthral me as I don't want to do cold, but I know houses and buildings stay warm. Despite this move, I'm sticking with this lad because it's also possible that after a year or three, the father will move on again, probably to a warmer, English-speaking, old Commonwealth country. (I use that phrase loosely.)

I'm still looking at maybe two to three of your human years. It's still going to be a walk-in and by that stage, Tom will be fifteen or sixteen. As a soul, it matters not to me whether he's in Canada or New Zealand or Timbuktu. His soul has agreed to this deal – because it is an arrangement between two souls – to give me space in this physical body.

I'm always mindful of Tobias who I use as a role-model almost. The lad concerned had an accident and was in the hospital. He was physically debilitated and unconscious for a while which made the walk-in invisible, seamless, from his human consciousness perspective. I like that model a lot and I observed that it worked extremely well. We still have to work out the circumstances as neither his soul nor I have any intent that Tom should suffer any long-term, bad physical effects.

So how have I been able to reach this irrevocable point? There has been a huge amount of discussion with all my guides up here including Daniel. He has seen bigger wisdom than I about the merits for me personally as well as for the world, in my coming back to do this. He, especially latterly, has provided very strong encouragement and support to talk through my concerns. I've had huge reservations (that's the best word) and I've had to slowly work through these and everyone has been fantastic. If I said, "What about this…?" there would be a discussion and I would see the merit in their answers or I would ask more questions.

Unbelievably patient and supportive, every single one of them. Nobody is saying, "Get a grip boy, and just do it..."

I've learnt an enormous amount just by watching and absorbing and being grateful for their patience and tolerance. Those are qualities I'm going to need in this coming life if I'm to influence world peace. World hatred flares in five seconds flat it seems but any achievements in world peace take an enormous amount of time and patience. Those qualities will transfer with me into my new life. Hopefully, I can sustain enough of them to make a difference on my soul path.

It seems to me that Tom's father could be a government official?

No. He's some sort of engineer who works for himself as a consultant. He will be employed by governments because he is highly regarded and they seek out his skills and knowledge and experience.

A foreign government, like the Canadian government, will offer him a contract on some big engineering project which would take several years. When that's finished he will then seek or be offered the next project.

As a family, they're happy with the idea of moving around. They've done it before and they quite enjoy the challenges of a new environment. The wife, the mother tries to get a bit of work when they're in these different places, mostly undemanding work simply because she knows that it's likely to be short-term. She has no interest in pursuing a great career but she has more than enough brain that she wants to engage it in a day-to-day sense. She will take on admin, office management-type roles in order to earn a few extra dollars but mainly to give her a focus, an occupation and mental stimulus.

Tom is now about fourteen and the parents are content with the one child. Father is far too busy with his work and work is all from his point of view. She's happy to be his support, his partner, keep the family going. She interacts a lot with Tom now that he's older and intelligent.

Dad takes enough time out to support the lad and Mum and Dad are a good pair in terms of their relationship. It's a good trio. Everybody is content with the way it works and all of them are pretty comfortable in their own company. It's mutually supportive and stable which is important for me. The experience of a family breakdown is certainly not part of my soul plan. Those qualities are partly why we've chosen this particular family.

You might ask why is it going to take two or three years? I don't want to do the teenage angst when the hormones start racing. But by fifteen or sixteen he's learnt to manage them to some degree, the brain is more developed and he's got a better idea of where he wants to go in terms of career or study.

Have you chosen your spirit guides?

Part of the planning process for everyone is to ask various souls to be their spirit guides. Absolutely and categorically, I could not have conceived of coming back without my parents from that last life being part of this. Later on, I was overwhelmed when my siblings also volunteered. They wanted to do it. They were clear that I had been very supportive of them in that life and they said, "If we can't help you then nobody can." Those four are the only ones with whom I have shared a life who are my spirit guides for my forthcoming incarnation.

I have about eight or ten additional senior beings up here, including Gabriel, who are also being my support team, which is just fantastic.

My new home

Ben   7 February 2015

I've been doing lots and lots of detailed planning including all the what-ifs, almost right through to Tom's death. You have to plan that far ahead before you come back. Part of this has been to liaise with Tom's existing soul.

I, any walk-in, need to work out a plan which meets the mutual needs of both souls. It's likely that his soul's needs and plan are not that far adrift from mine so that melding is not so difficult.

So now I'm saying that in the next year or eighteen months, I will be back on your earth-plane. Whether Tom is still in New Zealand by then – in a way it doesn't really matter too much. He's going to do all the things that teenage boys do...

Will he be aware that something is going to happen?

Unlikely. It is almost like fusion or this is how I understand it but I won't know till I've done it of course. My sense is that you just flow in like two bottles of water flowing together into one vessel. The lad won't know any different. As a human, you don't feel your soul anyway.

I would be communicating with Tom's soul and it would be aware that the timing is getting closer. I imagine there will be an incident where the physical is not operating fully normally, maybe a car accident or an illness that debilitates him. I will get the signal and I'll just blend in and off we go!

Nothing much else to report but I might try and come and talk to you just before I do the walk-in to tell you how I'm feeling about it all.

When you have done it we'd love to hear how that feels too.

After two thousand years out of the physical, you have to give me time to get used to being back. If I struggle, that leads to two possibilities. I will either be in and out so I could come back and tell you that, "I don't like this", or I might just settle and it might all work wonderfully well.

It's all a bit of a gamble.

Hopefully, we've minimised the gamble because we've done so much preparation. But the whole issue of free choice means we have no control and no ability to intervene. Even though we've tried to cover every possibility, it's hugely possible that we haven't in which case we will have to think on our feet and see what happens.

Tom's mates

Ben   20 February 2015

I'm not quite sure why but I have forgotten to tell you a bit about Tom's school friends because they are also part of why I chose Tom. He has four really close mates and they all share a passion for computers and technology.

They are not walk-ins; they are all straightforward one soul per physical body. They have all had more recent incarnations than I have, so they have more recent experience at living in the physical. That was partly why I needed to do a walk-in with someone who has also had more recent experience in the physical.

That planning has obviously included my host soul, because that will mean that, although there are five mates, there will be six souls. We all discussed it up here before they incarnated and we agreed that we would try and find humans in the same part of the world so we could hopefully be a mutual support team.

It's imminent...

Ben   18 March 2015

I wanted to talk to you now because this departure has become imminent, in the next few days I suspect. *Oooooo! I don't want to do this. I don't like this anymore. I want to chicken out.* I know I can't but I'm really not happy about this one jot. *Really* not happy.

What has happened that you have suddenly been propelled into incarnating so quickly? You thought it would be eighteen months or more.

To be honest, I'm not really sure. Something must have happened within my guiding group at some level – and I'm not privy to this – but I suddenly got the message that it needed to be very soon. Now whether that's something to do with me and my circumstances, whether it's something up here surrounding me, whether it's something that has affected other important people in this group who can't be available anymore. All of those are possibilities.

I'm fairly sure it's something of that ilk rather than anything to do with Tom. He's living his normal life, going to school and doing all the things lads do. It could be that his father has had notice that he needs to move soon. But I don't understand how that would affect me because the geography of where the recipient is living makes no difference.

My understanding is that it's something up here, likely in my planning group where things have changed for them which means they couldn't support me s for the next twelve or eighteen months or whatever. They've deemed it propitious that I go ahead, and having made the decision, there is an argument that says, "What are we waiting for? Let's just do it."

I just got the message that we'd better be doing this sooner rather than later. And it looks like being the next few days, the next week. *Ohhhh, deary me!*

Now, will I miss people up here? That's a good question. I will miss Hannah and Daniel given how much of our last life the three of us shared. I will miss them dreadfully.

When you come back up here you tend to go on your own path to a large extent and people who were important to you in the last incarnation on earth will be around when you first return. After that, you've all got your own things to be doing so you don't always maintain that closeness.

I'm sure I'll be happier once I'm there and I understand how the interaction with his existing soul works and how we're going to do everything. Some of that is planned but planning is one thing and doing is another altogether.

Thank you so much for coming this afternoon. I'm really grateful for that. I wish you both all the best in the coming years and I'm sure I'll be back while you are both still on this earth-plane. If it's all too horrible, then I guess I'll be back to tell you very soon. I'm sad to be leaving you both too.

Daniel   18 March 2015

We're going to miss him hugely. Sure, we can keep an eye and see what's going on but it's not the same as having him around the corner when you just want to chat. Of course, we all wish him *so* much luck. It's a big plan that he's set for himself. Whether he ends up being another Mark Gates, let's wait and see. It's possible.

Of course, we send him off with buckets of love and all our support and everything that we can muster for his next umpteen years wherever they will be.

Saint-Germaine   18 March 2015

I can't add anything to what has happened. I've not been part of that planning process, so I'm not privy to any of those considerations. I'm not aware, just from being around up here, of anything that would have made his departure imminent. We all wish him heaps of luck but I don't think he'll need it. It's a huge step, it's all new and after *so* long up here. Two thousand years is a long time to suddenly be propelled back into this earthly and from our perspective, dense, horrible way of existing, so it's no wonder he's got the collie-wobbles.

Tomorrow?

Ben   27 March 2015

Thank you so much for coming at such short notice. I've been getting *so* twitchy. I'm due to take up residence in the next day or two. I'm really, *really* stressed about this. I'm all edgy and I *really* wish I could find some way of not doing this. I don't think I can and if I tried I wouldn't get any gold stars from my support team. I realise that this would not serve any long-term good. Logically I know I need to do this but I am *so* stressed about it all.

Why am I so jittery all of a sudden? I suppose it's to do with it being so imminent. I now know that once I have walked in I have to have an extremely good reason for walking out again before the end. I suppose if I was to calm down a bit, I would say it's because it's all *so* unknown and so different and because I haven't had to do it for so, so long. Two thousand years is an awfully long time to not have to endure this… I remember Saint-Germaine saying it was yukky and dense and it's all of those things, all of which makes it less appealing as well.

Have I got anyone up here supporting me? Hannah and Daniel particularly, as well as some of my support team. Most of them have moved onto other things because there's nothing left to plan but a few of them will see me through right until I have left. It's a bit like seeing somebody off on a ship in your world. People come to the dock to wave you off until the ship has gone.

I'm so… not irritable but stressed, twitchy. I really, really, in my deepest heart, wish I hadn't agreed to do this. I suppose if I stop to think about it if I don't do it now, I'll have to do it another time, so let's get it over with. I know from up here that a whole lifetime down there will be nothing but a blink, but down there it will *not* be nothing. It will be long and protracted.

I don't quite know why I felt I had to come and tell you all that. Maybe I felt that you two would be supportive and it's part of the story. I can't say I'm conscious of other people I knew being this twitchy and stressed just before it's due to happen. Quite why I'm this bad, I don't really know. Being in this stewed state is not going to help the process. I have to calm down in order for the walk-in to work effectively and comfortably. We don't want the lad suddenly getting more ill or whatever because I've made such a mess of it. Whether that's likely, I don't know. But I need to really, really calm down.

I know there will be enjoyable and pleasant, really good times down there. If I think back I had loads of good times with Hannah and Daniel. Why I think there won't be this time, I have no idea. I'm being totally illogical about all this and really not helping myself. But it's a human reaction to get stressed about unknown things. I just thought I'd add that as a personal connection.

Oh dear, maybe I feel a bit better now having let off steam. Thank you for coming and listening.

It's not all bad here.

I guess part of the stress is this technology stuff. It's totally, totally alien and it changes so quickly too. I'm sure it's just a case of getting the hang of it. I do carry that same degree of intelligence forward into this coming life. That won't diminish. As this lad is already intelligent, then my added intelligence, *wow*... watch out world!

It's an opportunity to learn new things.

I'm sure I will. I think it's just this initial... I'm now just hanging around waiting. There's nothing much I can do because it's so short a time.

What's going to happen to the lad in the next couple of days? I think there is some sort of accident and that's the signal. Off I go.

He could be playing sport.

I don't have a sense of sport. The image I've got is walking, probably with his ear-thingies in, with his music or phone and he's not watching where he's going. He trips and bangs his head on the path. If you hit your head hard enough on concrete, you're going to lose consciousness, without doing any permanent damage, though. People around him will be concerned, get the ambulance and off he goes to the hospital. His parents will likely insist that he stays in until they are certain that he's OK. Once he's in hospital, that's my signal. I don't need to do the trauma bit. That's it. I shall be in New Zealand.

I'm sorry. I seem to have been venting a bit.

Don't worry. It's only human!

In that case, it's nice to have humans to listen to me and I'm sorry to have been in such a rush but I didn't quite know what else to do really.

That's fine. Come and talk to us anytime you like.

Thank you. It's really nice to know that. I don't think I have anything else to add so, in that case, I will say au revoir. I certainly will be back just to follow up on this and how I'm getting on, but I will just have to see how it goes.

Saint-Germaine   27 March 2015

Poor Ben! What a stew he's got himself into. I've never seen him like this. I suppose that if I was on the brink of having to reincarnate after such a long gap I would probably be equally twitchy. Even though I've only been gone a thousand years or thereabouts, so much has happened on your planet in that time, compared with the thousand years before. Of course, there was progress then but it was much slower than it has been in the last few hundred years. If I was in Ben's shoes, I guess I too would be beside myself. I have some empathy in a way. Being selfish, I'm glad it's not me that's about to return. I might remember that so I won't come back to this planet earth for a good long time, if ever.

Poor Ben. I might just see if I can find him and be a bit of comfort to him. Maybe it would be a nice parting gift.

Incarnate

Daniel   6 April 2015

He's gone. It's sad. We all knew that at some point he would reincarnate. He's been long in the planning so we knew quite a lot of detail about what he was hoping to achieve. But that doesn't make it any less sad now that he's actually gone. We can't communicate with him any more than you can. We too are at a loss to know how the walk-in went or how he's getting on.

It's literally been a week, a very short time but that doesn't mean we don't miss him up here. We would go for periods where we didn't see each other much but we three always knew that the others were there if we needed to.

Oh, it's sad but we know that a human life will be gone quick enough. But we still think of him and about him and wish all the best for him.

So just to confirm that he has definitely gone. He's more than intelligent. The lad he has gone into is intelligent and they will be absolutely fine.

Saint-Germaine   6 April 2015

Dear Ben. He was in such a pickle the other day. I did go and find him and put a big arm around his shoulder (is how you would understand it) to comfort him. He was very surprised but he quickly realised that I'd come because you had all been talking. He was really grateful. I stayed with him until he'd calmed down even more. He got himself back to a place of accepting and not being so worried and stressed. We talked for ages and I did my best to reassure him. I'm sure his planning would have covered most of the issues he was worried about and that he would learn while he was there – he didn't have to know all the answers before he left. I think that was basically what was he was getting bothered about, that it was all so uncertain. Anyway, he calmed down.

Other peoples' perspectives

Daniel   8 April 2015

Was Gabriel overseeing Ben's planning process?

Gabriel was definitely doing that. I was aware of him and probably the planning team was too.

Gabriel had had a role in guiding Ben in his last incarnation and this time he continued by trying to get Ben out of that seduction and back onto his soul-purpose path. Gabriel could sense that Ben was increasingly being seduced (his word) by your technology. He was increasingly being sucked into the idea of an incarnation so he could learn and play with it. As people kept saying, this was not a good enough reason for incarnating.

This planning process for any soul is like any planning process on earth. Firstly, you have to work out your objective or purpose. Once you've identified that you're going out to play football with the intent of winning, only then can you say that this is how we are going to play this particular game to achieve that end. But Ben was off playing in left field before he'd even worked out where the goal posts were.

Gabriel was trying to make him even identify the goal posts. Once you can see them at the far end of the field, there are still an infinite number of different tracks you can take to reach them. Then Ben had to come back and think about which path he was going to go down. You can incorporate the use of technology into many areas on your planet, so there are all sorts of things he could have chosen to do.

Gabriel was trying to influence without telling because it's none of our prerogatives to tell a soul what they can or can't do in an incarnation. You can only sow the seeds and guide. If Ben says he wants to build an aeroplane that will fly to the moon, then we will say that is fantastic but what about… Gabriel's influence would have been energy-driven but with a focus to get him to think about the bigger picture.

Gabriel   8 April 2015

Dear, dear Ben. What Daniel has said is right. I tried *really* hard to keep him focused on his soul needs for this new life.

He was like a little kid. "Ah, look at this!" He'd sit up here and watch something that you'd developed down there. "Look what this can do! Isn't this fantastic?" I remember him finding this little machine that you call a sat nav [a GPS]. "Isn't this fantastic!" and he would think back to his last life when he did a lot of travelling. "Just think if I'd had one of those things then. Wouldn't have that have been fantastic! *So* much easier." He was particularly seduced by sat navs but not to say he wasn't seduced by other things, lots of them.

I would say to him, "That's true but that life has long gone. What do you want a sat nav for in this one?"

"Er, all right. OK. I get the message," and he'd go away and think.

We went through this umpteen times. Then he'd see something else – he quite liked walkie-talkies. "Look, somebody over there can talk to me over here without me even seeing them and I can hear them. Isn't that fantastic." As for mobile phones – *well!* These were just to *die* for. All the things a modern mobile phone can do, *well*… He was hanging around Anthea when she got her new one. "Look at this…" and "look at that… I can't believe it." He was almost like, hopping on board as if there was going to be another walk-in there for a minute just so he could play with the technology.

"B-e-n… you've got to come back… It will all still be there when you get there but you have to think about the bigger issues."

"Er… O-K… I hear what you say."

He really was like a little kid. It was lovely to watch but we needed to do some serious planning here and without diminishing any ordinary person, he's a bit more serious and has got to have a big need before he can incarnate. Trying to get him back on track, oh, it was like trying to drag him out of a pot of chocolate. Deary me…

He'd come back contrite (that's the word) and we'd start to think a bit more about the planning then he'd see something else and off he'd go again. Ahhh! At times it was hard work, to be honest. It was a joy to watch at the same time… the enjoyment and the pleasure…

But over umpteen years, I've seen more than enough of them up here be seduced by something or someone on earth.

Digressing – in your European world, how many genius composers appeared on your planet in an incredibly short space of time, all extremely close to each other? Lots of them. They were all seduced. The first one went then the next one would, "listen to this…" and whoosh, he'd be gone. They went off like firecrackers, *bang, bang, bang.* It went on like that. From my moderately senior and therefore responsible position, to see all that happening … I was thinking, "Hang on. This is all getting out of control." We had to put some really big stoppers on it in ways that we don't normally do.

Having seen it in many, many souls – ordinary people too, not just the likes of the composers – who would get seduced, I'm very aware of the energy and the possibility of it happening. So when I saw Ben starting to get all excited and fired up about this technology, I thought, "oh-oh, gotta watch this one." I know how intelligent he is and that once he sees a challenge, he grabs it and wants to run with it. He couldn't see the possibility because, as he kept saying to you two, he didn't understand the technology. He could see what it would do. The sat nav would let him go anywhere without having to think about it, for example.

I could see how this seduction was happening. My job was to get him back even if it takes ten times or a hundred times.

We (me and others) had to encourage him to try and release this seduction without losing interest in the technology. I would say, "It's all going to still be there when you get there. It's only going to get bigger and better. You don't have to totally absorb it all before you go. But you cannot, you will not be allowed to go until you have worked out your bigger purpose, your personal needs and purpose and of course…" I had to keep reminding him, "It's not just you on a solo journey. You have to work with this lad's soul and get his agreement. If this is what you want to do, you can't just turn up. You have to plan it and be considerate of the host soul."

"Yeah, I know, I know, I know," and off he'd go again.

Finally, all of us gently got him back on the rails. Eventually, ages later, he came to one of the big planning meetings and very contritely said, "I want to offer my apologies to you all. I do now see how I've been like a little kid in a toy shop and I've only been half-listening to what you older and wiser folk have been trying to tell me. I want to thank you all for your patience and tolerance. I've now grasped what you've been trying to guide me towards all these many months. I just want to acknowledge that and thank you all. I will now focus on what I need to do, the detailed planning and my purpose."

We all just looked at each other and breathed a sigh of relief. "OK, we've succeeded!" Patience pays off in the end. From then on he was much more rational and balanced.

So now he's reincarnated to use technology to try to enhance peace in some part of the world at least. He sees that it has such potential for so many things. Because he spent his last life helping people he also brings that quality across with him to this life. Once he's learnt the technology then somehow, he's hoping that he can blend those two lines together. But that's now all done by human choice and within future technological developments. All we can do is sit and watch and wait. We have no more contact with him.

I'm back!

Ben   10 April 15

I'm sure you're all agog, like "what on earth am I doing coming back here this quick? It's daytime in New Zealand, so what am I doing floating around?"

Lots to tell. Did the walk-in go all right? Yes. What happened was that Tom did have a fall and banged his head rather hard on the concrete path. He was distracted by his earphones and music taking no notice whatsoever of the world around him. He bumped into somebody and then went down. It was quite a nasty bang on the head. Ambulance came. Took him to hospital. I think he might have lost consciousness briefly which is always a trigger for taking someone to the hospital. He was in for a couple of days and that's when I duly did my walk-in.

    I just slipped in. In your movies, you have ghosts that slide through walls. It was like that, a gentle wafting… like cigarette smoke wafts.

The fact that he was unconscious helps.

Yes, it did – good point. Two things. Firstly, physically his whole body and metabolism have calmed down; it's in a passive state. That then means, second thing, that there's no great resistance. If he's running down the street, the body is busy doing all the things it has to do to keep running. If he's lying, conscious or otherwise, in a hospital bed, he's silent and still and the bodily systems have settled down to a lower level of functioning (because that's all they need under those conditions) and the brain is not working optimally so even that has quietened down.

A good analogy would be slipping into a dead calm lake rather than a turbulent sea. If you were going swimming you know which is easier. That's what it was like. I now understand that's part of the reason for choosing somebody in a debilitated state. The walk-in was painless. It was seamless. It was as easy as and I now wonder why on earth I was getting so stressed about it beforehand.

Tom has fully recovered. Still taking it easy. His mother's been a bit worried and has been keeping an alert eye out for him. But he's gently getting back to normal and now he's walking down the street again with his earplugs in. I mean, what can you say? He's a lad. They do these things.

Tom's host soul was very welcoming. I know we'd done all this early planning and I had to communicate with his soul in order to make it all happen.

At the moment, we're both operating separately from each other within the physical Tom. Whether we remain separated or whether we merge is too early to say. It's possible to do both. If we stay separate, we must not conflict, because that sets up all sorts of peculiar situations in the physical.

So how am I floating out right now in the middle of the afternoon? When there are two of us you can do this. Tom's original soul is looking after the home front and I'm out here talking to you.

I hope that I will have happy times and I have a greater sense now that it will be a happy time. In another few months, I will really laugh about what a stew I got into before I came.

Anyway, this is very likely to be the last goodbye for a very long time. I know I have said it before but I am infinitely grateful to both of you for staying with me through this journey and for all the work that is yet to come before this can be a published book. Thank you, thank you! And on that note, it really is goodbye.

Daniel   10 April 15

We were sitting up here listening to that with great interest. I don't have any direct line of communication with him so we were really pleased to hear that he's happy and settling in and no longer feels great angst or upset about the whole thing. That was very comforting.

Gabriel   10 April 15

I was very pleased to hear that Ben is now happier in himself. I don't have any communication with him either.

Well, there is nothing more that we can tell you. We can only wish him every success with his objectives; the planet certainly needs all the help it can get towards peace.

However, there is the possibility that later on Ben might be able to come back and give us further updates which we can publish as a sequel but this is unlikely to be for many years yet.

While we are waiting we should explore a bit deeper into other peace initiatives that have happened on earth over recent years.

Chapter 9
PEACE ON EARTH...

Because Ben has peace as his goal for this new life, we were prompted to ask about other initiatives in this direction. This is what we were given by Saint-Germaine.

When did the new-age era or concept start?

If you went back into the 1800s and earlier, of course, there were wars and these would be like Napoleon with his soldiers who fought on the battlefield. Before that, the Spanish, Portuguese, Dutch and English were fighting on the high seas for the domination of new lands. These battles would be fought by the sailors. Ordinary folk at home weren't particularly affected by any of these and they were also living in societies which were much more community-focused. If you were at the poverty end of the spectrum, you helped your neighbours. If you were at the affluent end, you helped by employing people and you would be seen to do good. Britain, America, Europe would all have had community-focused lifestyles then.

Through the 1900s, we had the two World Wars and every other conceivable war ever since. Both of these wars hugely affected locals. Not only did all the men go off to fight, leaving the women behind to look after and feed the family, but as the war progressed, countries became more impoverished and it was more difficult to feed the family. These wars had a direct impact on ordinary folk.

Through the Second World War, there were people who chose not to sign up and they were called pacifists. After the Second World War, there were ongoing wars in South-East Asia, mainly Korea, Malaya and Vietnam. Once Vietnam started there was a big backlash in the form of conscientious objectors.

Even in the First World War where it was totally unacceptable to refuse to go, people would choose roles like ambulance drivers or medical people, ie roles that were not fighting. They too were pacifists even if they didn't use that word but it was manifesting in these various forms. So there are these longstanding roots of peace initiatives which come through history as the basis for this new-age movement.

You could ask – what is going on in the souls of the pacifists and conscientious objectors and those who followed, like the Greenham Common women in England protesting against local nuclear activities? What is going on in the souls of these folk who so actively refuse to go to war?

Their souls all have a huge pacifist element in their energy bubble and it's strong enough for them, as adult humans, to let it come to the fore and say that I'm not going to participate in this war. From that comes phrases like 'peace not war' and 'love not war,' and actions that continued on and expanded out to become what you see as the new-age world.

These days there is a lot more affluence in virtually every Western society to support new-age practitioners like masseurs, reiki or crystal healers or any alternative health modality. These things could only emerge once society had recovered post-war and moved into the 1960s and beyond, where the men had returned and jobs were producing more money. Through the '60s there was also the Flower Power movement which was part of the same thing.

Now you could ask – have we up here, gone back that far, one hundred and twenty or more years to the early 1900s, to start sending out waves of different souls in the hope of generating peace? People who would try to wave the peace flag in their societies and the answer is yes.

The likes of Florence Nightingale and ambulance men in the trenches of the First World War were all early attempts on our part to generate different parallel streams of peace-makers.

Our logic was that we had to create enough of these streams, in different cultures and we needed to keep topping them up in some fashion. We could see the potential for the First World War looming and it didn't take too long after that to recognise that Hitler wasn't going to be a happy chappy.

As a strategic plan, we encouraged souls which had a high percentage of this quality of care and pacifism, to incarnate. This was to try to get different streams of people all over the world who would keep on waving their flag for peace. If enough of them did it for long enough, there would be enough momentum that peace would ensue.

All of that was done through Western, Christian-based societies. Then, of course, Asian powers, particularly China and Russia have become significant in the world, so we started to think about how we could put these peace-streams of souls into their communities. As you will be aware, there are plenty of Russian and Chinese musicians who are extraordinarily skilled. There is also an enormous number of Chinese and Russian athletes these days. You only have to look at the nationalities in any Olympic Games. If you went back to the 1950s and '60s, these competitors were largely white and Anglo but today they are largely not white and not Anglo. Not too many peak athletes or musicians pick up guns in later life. Again, this is another way of trying to generate peace in some fashion.

I'm conscious of the ex-Olympian lady[10] on Australian television who does the ads for a foot massager. That is quite small but it is still significant because it is a peaceful and self-healing product and message, and because it's a television advertisement, lots of people are seeing it. Even now in her late seventies, she is, probably unconsciously, still promoting this health activity which is peaceful and loving.

I have talked about methods of trying to generate peace on earth but as Gabriel said right at the beginning, people are petrified of death and we want to allay that fear. In a broader sense over the last hundred years, death has increasingly come from atrocities, Islamic fundamentalist and war-based atrocities. We want to reassure ordinary folk by letting them know that for at least one hundred and twenty years, we up here have been very subtly infiltrating different types of folk in little patches all over the planet, to try and engender more emphasis on peace.

To use your human phrase, there is strength in numbers. The 1960s Flower Power movement was a gorgeous example of all kinds of people who were dropping out. But they were only dropping out to do peaceful things and were really living love-thy-neighbour even if it was drug-driven. We have been working for all these years to infiltrate – and you can use that word – different streams into those parts of the world that were likely to become involved in war; to motivate more people in those populations to get a movement going, which had an underlying, if subconscious, theme of peace.

---

[10] Dawn Fraser – the first woman swimmer to win gold medals in three consecutive Olympics (1956, 1960, 1964).

Now in this context, the most *fantastic* thing, which has come to the fore in recent years, is the internet-based activist websites[11] for protesting against bad things. Some of these now have millions, if not tens of millions, of followers. They will put up a campaign usually in the form of a petition (although occasionally there is an appeal for money) which costs five seconds of a person's life to read and sign using only their email address. These folk have been fabulously successful in getting all sorts of huge, negative, manipulative, mostly big corporates but also some governments, to reverse some of the actions where they are screwing impoverished third-world countries often for logging timber or mining for natural resources. They will name-and-shame these organisations which are, no question, abusing societies. One story (among many) from AVAAZ to illustrate:

> In early 2014, our community decided on one crazy goal -- to deliver the largest mobilisation on climate change in history, with thousands marching through New York calling for leaders to act.
>
> On September 21, it actually happened.
>
> Working closely with our friends at 350.org and 1,700 other organisations, over 400,000 people marched through Manhattan and hundreds of thousands more rallied in over 2,000 communities around the world. It was a beautiful expression of our love for all that climate change threatens and an expression of hope that we can build a world powered by 100% clean energy.

---

[11] For example, AVAAZ (avaaz.org), GetUp! (getup.org.au), SumOfUs (sumofus.org), CommunityRun (communityrun.org), Amnesty International (amnesty.org). There are many others.

Over 18 ministers marched and Avaaz Executive Director Ricken Patel presented a 2 million strong petition to UN Secretary-General Ban Ki-moon on the march in New York, calling for 100% clean energy worldwide.

The marches led to many leaders at the following UN summit acknowledging the pressure coming from the streets with Barack Obama saying, "our people keep marching, we have to answer their call." The pressure is working -- less than two months after the march, the US and China signed a landmark agreement, including new targets for carbon emission reductions by the US and a first-ever commitment by China to stop its emissions from growing by 2030.

Now in 2015, leaders are now starting to act with Germany pushing the 100% clean target at the G7 and the initial draft of the Paris text committing to decarbonise the planet.

These are the most fabulous benefits to come from the internet that we certainly never anticipated. The folk who started these sites have all got this same strong pacifist streak.

In bygone days, groups like the Greenham Common ladies could only set up camp, wave their flags and get heard mainly through the media. These days these websites can sign up millions and millions of supporters in a very short space of time and deliver their petitions very effectively with stunning successes. These are just the best ever mechanisms in our view for helping move peace along. I don't mean just in a war sense but in the sense of corporate greed and aggression.

Why do some youngsters vividly remember and recount their most recent past life? Why these particular children and not others?

Good question. In the future, these children are likely to be significant in this new age or spirituality or esoteric arena. Giving them this head start is to give them a flavour of the whole subject particularly for past lives and reincarnation. My observation is that once they reach the age of eight or nine or ten, they mostly forget which is totally understandable and is the way that the body was designed to operate.

The fact that they can articulate this life so clearly comes from that element in their soul energy bubble where they store their past life memories. This is particularly strong so that they could and would remember this most recent life. There is obviously a connection from the soul to the remembering part of the brain and then the articulating part of the brain.

These children have usually come back very quickly, by which I mean ten or twenty years not hundreds. Very often they died in their youth, often unexpectedly, sadly quite often through violence, otherwise through ill health or accidents. By 'youth' I mean anywhere from say five to fifteen or eighteen. To illustrate:

> At around the age of four, Jalen started talking about his "other family." Initially, his parents took no notice but he persisted until eventually, they heard the whole story.
>
> In that life, he had two siblings and his brother then had the same name as his sister in this life. His name then was also Jalen although the surname was different. He was very clear that his parents then were not the same people as his parents today.

At the age of seventeen, he was attacked and stabbed in the forearm just below the elbow. He was taken to the hospital and "the blood was put back in" (his phrase). He obviously survived for a while because at the age of eighteen, "I shrunk back to baby-size."

Generally dying like that isn't part of their soul plan so mostly they've come back again to repeat the same plan and goals but like everyone else, they have forgotten their objectives. Because the previous life was abruptly truncated the soul plan was already in place; they didn't have to go through years of planning it all out. In Jalen's story, you can see the parallels with same-name siblings.

These are pretty much always ordinary youngsters, ie they're not prodigies, they not super-bright at anything, and they return into ordinary families all over the world. As a rule, their memories are crystal clear. They have no sense of questioning why; they just say that this is what happened.

This is not a new phenomenon; it's probably been going on for thirty or forty years. We're hoping – that's all we can do because human free-will will intervene later – that when they become adults and chose their paths in life, that these past-life remembrances will stick with enough of them to encourage them to become interested and active in this world you call new age – in any form; we don't care. It's another mechanism for trying to bring some peace to the world. You can't show me too many new-age practitioners who are out there waving guns around. That's the whole purpose from our point of view.

What is going on with indigo children who were born through the 1970s, crystal children who were born through the 1990s and millennium and rainbow children who are being born now?

All of these children are yet another prong at trying to generate future peace. They have come back in tranches and there are not heaps of them. For every indigo or crystal or rainbow child, there will be a thousand ordinary children. They are mostly in the Western world; they have above-average sensitivities to people and new age-type things.

It's yet another way of trying to bring in streams of people who can hopefully espouse and enact peace in any shape or form in their adulthood. They will all be hugely strong pacifists. By bringing them in waves, you've got one tranche followed by the next and then the next, who will go out and become new-age practitioners like perhaps past-life regressionists or work with crystals or become masseurs, all caring, gentle, pacifist, healing activities which are all part of a people- and community-focused lifestyle. If you are practising any of those you are giving to the community and that's the whole point.

So far you have had several tranches and there will probably be more. The different tranches work like waves rolling onto a beach; one comes and does what it does and the next one follows doing the same thing, and so that momentum continues.

Ben

Let me offer the last words on this. I can't possibly be the only human on this planet who has an agenda to help towards peace on earth. So I hope that linking this last chapter to my story will bring greater understanding and benefits.

Epilogue

Clynton and I have hugely enjoyed this journey. We both started out with what we thought was a fairly good understanding of this whole subject, but we have learnt heaps more than we ever anticipated – and we feel very privileged and blessed to have been part of this process.

In conclusion, as Saint-Germaine said at the end of our many Q&A sessions, "I can't believe that one person could have thought of so many complicated questions. But I'm really happy because that is going to make this book far more interesting, give it far more depth and almost an added dimension."

As Gabriel said right at the end, "We genuinely want to spread the word. So many people are petrified of death and we want to allay that fear by reassuring them that life continues afterwards."

We all really hope that we have achieved both of these or at the very least gone some way towards reassuring you about life after death.

About the Author

Anthea Wynn is a channeller and author with an eclectic range of co-authored and best-selling publications including *Aged Care Homes, the complete Australian guide* (2008) and *Principles and Practice of Consumer Credit Risk Management* (2001). These reflect her equally eclectic careers (in both the UK and Australia) covering radiography, computer programming, consumer credit risk management, marketing communications and now channelling, writing and publishing. You can see more about her softer side at http://celestialrevelations.com/about/.

Anthea is a member of the Australian Society of Authors, Australian Publishers Association and the Victorian Spiritualist Union. She lives in Melbourne, Australia.

Acknowledgements

My first and largest thank you goes to both Ben and Saint-Germaine without whom none of this would ever have come to pass. While I know that they have really enjoyed this journey, that doesn't alter my gratitude for their hours of continuing input and willingness to answer all our questions. Likewise, our thanks go to both Gabriel and Daniel for their alternate perspectives which give a wider dimension to the whole story.

On this earthly plane, I couldn't have done any of this channelling without Clynton Cooper-Alyn, my facilitator, my prop and never-flagging support even through the period when he was himself experiencing life-threatening problems.

I have had considerable help from Pam Holland and various good folk at fiverr.com with the typing. My beta-readers were Peter Benn, Rosalba Gustin and Peter Campbell all of whom came up with terrific questions and pointed out places where better explanations were needed. Simon Surtees was the inspiration for the questions on twins, particularly identical twins. Danielle Taylor, a professional past-life regressionist, contributed some of the stories from her clients' experiences. To all of you, an enormous thank you, and heaps of gratitude is flowing your way.

Now two other humans have gone out of their way, well above any hope or expectations on my part, to help with two particularly big obstacles. I potentially had problems with an existing trademark which prevented me using Saint-Germaine's other, better known, name and Leonie Loveday went way above the call of duty in getting legal advice for me for which I am still indebted.

The other good lady was Michelle Madden, my editing teacher during my recent Diploma of Professional Writing and Editing, who encouraged and supported me by providing the opportunity, and thus the confidence, to speak openly about my channelling work. This had been a big hurdle for me and Michelle was a huge catalyst in my being able to overcome this, for which I can never say thank you enough.

Lastly, I need to add that all the stories quoted here are true but some names have been changed to protect individual privacy.

www.ingramcontent.com/pod-product-compliance
Lightning Source LLC
Chambersburg PA
CBHW020422010526
44118CB00010B/376